50 years of

COVENANT MARRIAGE

God wrote our love story :

Moving our marriage from

Good to Great

to

Built to Last

Let Him write yours

ChuDace Publishing
3540 E. Broad St. Suite 120-192
Mansfield, Texas 76063, U. S. A.

©   2019 by ChuDace Publishing

ISBN: 9780998584379 [Print Edition]

Published and printed in the United States of America

Marriage is lifetime work in progress, with blessings and burdens. A great marriage can only come from great perseverance; and nothing in the world can replace perseverance. Never quit ! Winners never quit and quitters never win.

DEDICATION

We dedicate this book to our children, our most precious blessings of inestimable value:

Rotimi & Banke

Tony & Rayo

Lanre & Busola

Ayokunle & Venessa

&

our beautiful grandchildren.

Our greatest blessing is the way God has nurtured, promoted and protected our friendship, courtship and marital relationship for nearly sixty years, and the inestimable joy of being living witnesses to efforts by our children in parenting their own off-springs in line with the teachings of Christ. May the Lord continue to provide all that you need to excel beyond our imaginations.

ACKNOWLEDGEMENTS

The inspiration to write this book came from many sources, notably our long experience in managing a marital relationship for five decades in real time, personal experiences of other married couples around us, and the rich, spiritually inspiring teachings of experienced pastoral ministries that we have listened to for many years. We wish to acknowledge in particular: Love Worth Finding Ministries (Adrian Rogers); John Hagee Ministries; Marriage Today Ministries (Jimmy & Karen Evans); Powerpoint Ministries (Jack Graham); JoyceMyer Mininstries; Crossroads Christian Church (Barry Cameron); Hour of Power Ministries (Bobby Schuller); Leading the Way Ministries (Michael Youssef); TDJakes Ministries. We also acknowledge the inspiration gained from reading the bestseller "When God writes your love story: Experience the ultimate adventure" by Eric and Leslie Ludy. We encourage couples who wish to grow their marital relationship from good to great, built to last a lifetime and those struggling in their marriage to take full advantage of these and many other very useful resources that are widely available. We hope also that this contribution from a seasoned couple, based mainly on our experience in navigating through nearly sixty years (courtship and marriage) of richly fulfilling journey together will be a source of inspiration to those coming behind us, and inspire in them the conviction that, with God's blessing and perseverance, marriages can be happy, great and built to last a lifetime.

PREFACE:
GOD WROTE OUR LOVE STORY

Most people write memoirs which chronicle their life achievements, and we have quite a few we could write about considering that we have lived this long and reached the pinnacle of our respective professional careers. However, we decided to share experiences from our fifty eight years of relationship and fifty years of marital bliss, enriched by the varied experiences of others around us who have had successful marriages, and of those who have not been so lucky, because we consider all central to understanding the institution of marriage and what needs to be done to make a marriage work. We believe also that building a great marriage and family life on solid Christian and moral values, thereby creating a stable home front has been the foundation of all our other individual and joint life achievements. Many other couples with similar values who believe that a good marriage is a precursor to many other achievements in life have also been equally or even more successful.

In a phenomenally successful book: *When God writes your love story*, Eric and Leslie Ludy established the exceptional values of letting God take control of your love life from the beginning. After fifty years of a great marriage, we have a testimony: it works wonders!! We had known each other as family friends for over a decade but started dating in our late teens. We were both totally inexperienced in the art of dating, nothing beyond platonic relationships. However, it was like we both heard a Divine voice saying *"this is going to be your beloved in whom you will be well pleased"*. Niyi made the move in 1960, (he was twenty), Simi responded positively (she was sixteen), and we have not looked back ever since. We were both fortunate to have been raised in Christian homes and we both brought very strong Christian dating values to the relationship. Over the next two years we saw each other fairly frequently and spent most of the time getting to know each other, consolidating our faith, jointly planning our future careers. The following five years were trying times because we were separated due to the pursuit of our educational goals, but one fact was evident: we both believed we had found our soulmate through Divine guidance, and distance would not surmount God's will. Through prayers, joint planning and against all odds, we both ended up as graduate students in Birmingham, United Kingdom in 1967 and got married a year later.

People ask all the time how we were able to sustain interest in each other over eight years of dating and courtship, and still behave as *just married* after fifty years of cohabiting. The answer is simple: we both believe that the mutually spontaneous interest in each other was Divinely-inspired, we made God the foundation of the relationship from the beginning, and we let Him write our story to date. From the beginning we developed and nurtured a number of core values which we believe were largely responsible for the success of our journey so far: partnership, total mutual commitment to the relationship, empathy, perseverance, selflessness, trust and respect. We opened our first joint bank account as graduate students (either to sign) a year before we got married, and the model has not changed to date. It was a clear demonstration of mutual trust and total mutual commitment to the relationship, and an early establishment of the role money was going to play in our marital life - an indispensable servant (not master). We both worked very hard to grow family wealth and establish a co-pilot family management model whereby either could take full control seamlessly if and when necessary.

Eric and Leslie wrote such an authentic book which has been a source of inspiration to millions of young lovers, hopefully, our account based mostly on the experience in our relationship will be a good complement, especially for those who have already embarked on the journey through marital life and are dealing in real time with the myriads of associated problems and issues. We do not claim that our model fits all, in fact, we believe ours was *made to measure and was tested again and again.* Go to the Supreme Designer for yours!! While this book gives few details of our experiences in our journey through marital life, the views expressed on core issues in marriage emanate from our real life experiences and those of people around us in dealing with the numerous challenges and trials in the pathway to building a happy and sustainable marital relationship. Our work has also been complemented by extensive research of published literature across different cultures. Statistics show that only about five to six percent of married couples live to celebrate their fiftieth wedding anniversary, therefore we consider ourselves richly blessed and feel obliged to share our experiences and testimonies. We hope that our message resonates strongly with others coming behind us.

For over forty years, we lived in a closely-knit, faith-based academic community which placed as much emphasis on building rich learning institutions as on promoting the family institution. In this book, we share those pro-marriage and pro-family values that couples may find useful in resolving many critical issues that will inevitably arise: personal sacrifices, optimal choice of abode, growing a great relationship, career issues, managing external relationships, raising children, growing family wealth, and many more. We have seen many marriages progress from ***good to great, built to last a lifetime***; we have also seen promising marriages collapse before the first anniversary due to avoidable mistakes. While we appreciate the fact that there is no template that works for every marriage, in our experience and those of many others, there are many common values that help build happy and lasting relationships, while there are also many common mistakes that help break up marriages.

There are always many factors in and out of a marital 'comfort zone' and in the society at large which require quick, constructive, and united responses for a marriage to survive. We share these varied experiences, hopefully for the benefit of those who are struggling in their relationships, but more especially for those who are just 'joining the club' or are yet to start a relationship, since it is always better to avoid than mitigate a mistake. We take an inter-generational perspective, focusing on our generation and those after us including our children and friends who are married and are growing their own families. Having lived in other countries and cultures for a significant part of our fifty years of marriage and gained much wider experiences, we reflect this cross-cultural perspective which could significantly touch the lives of those who would read this book. We focus on the hallmark of our Christian Heritage which inspired us to start off our relationship with *Christ as the cornerstone* fifty eight years ago. It drew us close to each other; it helped us to adjust to and accommodate each other; it shielded us and ours from darkness and external interference; it enriched our understanding of the varied and changing scenes of life and helped us to develop coping strategies; and it shaped our aspirations and expectations in the course of trying to build a great marriage.

We would like to share our experience on how our heritage brought us blessings and how the blessings deepened with more exposure to *Jesus, The Way, The Truth and The Life,* to wisdom, understanding, knowledge, faith, hope, love derived from the Word of God. The Word says *"We are seated in Him, high above all these things having been raised together, and made to sit together in heavenly places in Christ Jesus"* (Ephesians 2:6).

A great marriage is everybody's dream but there is no blessing without a burden: adversities, challenges, persecution, sacrifices. Building a good marriage and moving to a great marriage, built to last starts and ends with the grace of God, but there is a lot that couples can do to improve their chances of reaching the promised land: *a great marital relationship for life.* This book primarily targets Christians but most of the core values discussed apply equally to non-Christians and, hopefully, all who read it will find something useful in their quest to build a happy, enduring and lasting marital relationship.

Niyi & Simi Afonja

ABOUT THE AUTHORS

Simi and Niyi both grew up in the small, closely-knit town of Ado-Ekiti in the old Western State of Nigeria in the 1940s. For many years, the two families remained good friends but destiny changed all that, and the rest is history. Friendship from their late teens grew into courtship over eight years, education and career goals were planned jointly and both ended up on doctoral programs in Birmingham, United Kingdom, Simi in Sociology and Niyi in Engineering. The knot was tied in Birmingham in August 1968 and both joined the academic staff of University of Ife (now Obafemi Awolowo University) on the same date in December 1969. Both retired after forty years of very rich academic and consulting career profiles which included many international visiting fellowships and consultancies, and are now based in Texas, U.S.A. The union is blessed with children and grandchildren.

Spirit-Filled, Spirit-led Marriage

"Unless the Lord builds the house, the builders labor in vain."
Psalm 127:1

Marriage is a spiritually binding covenant between husband and wife before God who designed the first marriage and gave away the first bride, with very specific instructions: *"Therefore a man shall leave his father and his mother and hold fast to his wife, and they shall become one flesh"* (Genesis 2:24). It is noteworthy that God created woman from man thereby making two out of one, and then merged two into one flesh by marriage. In effect, marriage is designed as an indivisible entity rooted in a mutual commitment that can withstand the most tempestuous storms. God designed marriage as a mutually beneficial partnership with distinct roles and complementary responsibilities for each partner. The teachings of Apostle Paul (Ephesians 5:22-33) expanded this divine doctrine on marriage by exhorting both husband and wife to walk in the Spirit and have a spirit-filled marriage as a prerequisite for growing a happy, resilient and lifelong marriage. To achieve this, each partner needs to nurture a strong personal relationship with God. Only then can couples have a spirit-filled, spirit-led marriage that guides them safely through the numerous challenges, trials and tribulations they will face throughout their marriage, "till death do them part."

Growing a strong personal relationship with God and strong relationship with each other invites the guidance of the Holy Spirit in growing a selfless, sacrificial relationship and cultivating mutual submission; it helps consolidate a covenant of partnership, mutual faithfulness, respect, empathy, self-denial, and mutual support. A spirit-filled and spirit-led marriage that keeps God at the center of the relationship helps cultivate a truly conjugal love, sanctifies the home and opens the doors for God to bless the home in many amazing ways. A married couple who experiences the blessings of the Holy Spirit will notice their love increasing with each passing day, regardless of the trials they may encounter. Decades into their marriage, they will still find joy in making each other happy.

A spirit-filled marriage is one that is controlled and empowered by the Spirit of God, one in which there is total submission to God and to each other. It means giving up one's independent rights and replacing personal interests with family interests. Submitting to one another does not imply inferiority, it is in obedience to God; it implies nurturing sacrificial love for each other, one that eliminates selfishness and cultivates enduring partnership, mutual empathy, mutual respect, perseverance, a strong feeling of goodwill toward each other and the will to meet each other's deepest needs. In a spirit-filled marriage, partners find that, as they get closer to God, they also get closer to one another. They find that the Spirit brings a divine dimension to their marriage, transforms their way of thinking and helps them grow mutual true love born of the Holy Spirit which better equips them to navigate and manage the numerous trials, tests and crises in their journey together through life. No marriage, not even a Christian marriage is immune from crises that can bring their marriage to the brink of collapse: you will go through many struggles in your marital relationship and face many personal and family crises, but you find that, through it all, your love for each other will grow stronger and bind you closer, and you will marvel at the gift God gave you in each other. Submitting your marriage to God's plan will refine and increase your commitment to one another and empower you to jointly confront forcefully the numerous and inevitable battles ahead. Couples take an oath to stick together for better, for worse, it is helpful to note that, quite often, the better comes after the worse.

Marriage is divinely designed to be fireproof. It doesn't mean fire will not come but when it does, a Spirit-led couple will be fully equipped to deal with it.

Your marriage can grow from good to great,
built to last a lifetime only if both leave home
and become one.

TABLE OF CONTENTS

Dedication……………………………………....……………… iv

Acknowledgements……………………………………....…… v

Preface: God wrote our love story…………....……………… vi

About the authors……....………………………………....…… xi

The Spirit-Filled Marriage xii

Highlights……………………………………....……………… xxi

Marriage quotes……………………………………....………… xxix

1. Marriage is a Divine institution……………....…… 1

    1.1   INTRODUCTION……………………………….... 1

    1.2   MARRIAGE IS GOOD………………………….…. 6

    1.3   THE PENTACORES (FIVE CORES) OF A
             SUCCESSFUL MARRIAGE……………………… 9

2. Choice of partner, dating and courtship….. 13

    2.1   INTRODUCTION…………………………………. 13

    2.2   MODERN DATING AND COURTSHIP………… 14

    2.3   CHRISTIAN COURTSHIP…………………….… 17

    2.4   CHOOSING A LIFE PARTNER………………… 22

            2.4.1   Does pedigree matter?………………… 22

            2.4.2   Right age for marriage……………… 24

            2.4.3   Risk factors…………………………... 26

    2.5   GETTING TO KNOW YOU: REALLY?……….... 29

    2.6   PRAYING AS A DATING COUPLE…………… 30

3. The marriage ceremony……………… 33

    3.1   INTRODUCTION…………………………………. 33

    3.2   THE MARRIAGE CEREMONY………………… 34

    3.3   WHAT'S IN A NAME?……………………… 37

    3.4   CHOOSING POST-MARITAL ABODE………… 38

4. Startup: getting to know each other and building a great marriage on a solid Christian foundation...... 41

4.1 INTRODUCTION.............. 41
4.2 BECOMING ONE FLESH............. 42
4.3 THE POWER OF A PRAYING FAMILY.......... 43
4.4 COMPATIBILITY IN MARRIAGE............. 46
4.5 ADJUSTMENT AND ACCOMMODATION.......... 47
4.6 CONFLICT RESOLUTION............. 51
4.7 MANAGING ANGER AND MALICE.......... 52
4.8 COMMUNICATION.............. 55
4.9 LEADERSHIP BY EXAMPLE.......... 56
4.10 GENDER ROLES IN MARRIAGE........... 57
4.11 LAYING A SOLID FOUNDATION FOR A HAPPY MARRIAGE........... 58
4.12 MANAGING FAMILY WEALTH.......... 63
4.13 FAITH AND FINANCE............ 66
4.14 PREPARING FOR RETIREMENT........... 70
4.15 SEX IN MARRIAGE............ 71
4.16 MANAGING MIDLIFE CRISIS........... 75

5. Raising children and parenting...... 77

5.1 INTRODUCTION.............. 77
5.2 RAISING CHILDREN............ 78
5.3 PARENTING............. 80
    5.3.1 Parenting skills............ 81
    5.3.2 Killing your child softly with love.......... 81
    5.3.3 Parenting style........... 82
    5.3.4 Child discipline............ 84
    5.3.5 Shared parenting............ 87
    5.3.6 Do as I do, not as I say.......... 89
    5.3.7 Managing Work-Parenting challenges.......... 90

6. **Potential pitfalls in marriage**............................. 93

   6.1   INTRODUCTION.. 93

   6.2   MARRIAGE IS SMOOTH SAILING?
          BRACE YOURSELVES FOR HURRICANES,
          TORNADOES AND TSUNAMIS......................... 93

   6.3   LIVING APART: LEAD US NOT INTO
          TEMPTATION.. 99

   6.4   MANAGING EXTERNAL INTERFERENCE........... 100

   6.5   DEALING WITH IN-LAWS................................ 102

   6.6   INFIDELITY... 109

   6.7   ABUSE... 111

   6.8   DIVORCE... 111

7. **Great marriages can last a lifetime**................. 119

   7.1   INTRODUCTION.. 119

   7.2   THE FINAL YEARS... 119

   7.3   COMPLACENCY.. 121

   7.4   SELFISHNESS... 122

   7.5   BECOMING GRANDPARENTS............................ 123

   7.6   HARVEST TIME: IT IS NOT ALL ABOUT MONEY............... 123

   7.7   PREPARING FOR THE INEVITABLE.................................... 124

8. **REFERENCES AND BIBLIOGRAPHY**.......... 125

CORE ISSUES IN MARRIAGE

❖ Christ needs to be the cornerstone and foundation of your marriage, all other ground is sinking sand.

❖ The marriage institution is great and ordained by God.

❖ Intimacy, passion empathy and commitment. (Cornerstones of a happy marriage).

❖ Partnership, sharing, mutual support and complementation. (Prerequisites for a happy and successful marriage).

❖ Adjustment, accommodation, communication. (Vital relationship management tools).

❖ Building a joint force against external interference and attacks.

❖ Conflict and problem resolution skills.

❖ Raising children and parenting.

❖ Building and nurturing family wealth.

KEY INDICATORS OF A HAPPY MARRIAGE

❖ They are grateful to God.

❖ They forgive and forget.

❖ They are each other's best friend and cheerleader.

❖ They are realistic and know that neither is perfect.

❖ They trust each other completely.

❖ They have spirited and purposeful conversations.

❖ They accept each other's differences and help nurture each other's assets rather than dwell on the weaknesses.

❖ They know that marriage is a lifetime work in progress.

❖ They know that marriage is about partnership; shared responsibilities and mutual respect and readjustment; selflessness.

*The highest happiness on earth is the happiness
of a successful marriage.*

Highlights

❖ Marriage is good. To build a great marriage you need God's favor, deep friendship, lots of love, hard work, mutual resilience, adaptivity, tolerance, respect, and selfless commitment to each other. With persistence and perseverance, you can move your marriage from good to great and build a relationship that will last a lifetime. Nothing good ever comes easy and blessings and burdens are soulmates. Marriage comes from heaven, so is thunder and lightning. The road to well of happy and successful marriage passes through well of conflict, well of argument, well of persecution, well of opposition, well of temptation, well of obstacles. Expect joy and happiness, difficulties, trials and tribulations as you navigate the tortuous journey through all the changing scenes of life. Be determined to surmount all obstacles at all costs, and you will reap lots of fulfillment, rewards and blessings at the end of the tunnel.

❖ In order to build and grow a great marriage that will last a life time, couples need God's grace and mutual, unflinching commitment to their marital vows to   navigate the long, exciting, tortuous, tumultuous, and mined road to a resilient, happy, lasting marriage: *"to have and to hold, from this day forward, for better, for worse, for richer, for poorer, in sickness and in health, to love and to cherish, till death do us part, according to God's holy ordinance"*. Work together with intimacy, passion and commitment, and the ultimate rewards are heavenly.

❖ Your partner is ridden with faults, so are you !! Look a little closer and you will see a large reservoir of assets that can be nurtured, (with your help, understanding and support) to bring out the best in your partner. When God created Eve, He did not set out to create another Adam, (otherwise He would have molded her in clay), rather, He created a partner to compensate for Adam's deficiencies and make up for what he lacked. He wanted to create something different, yet equally a masterpiece. Clearly, Eve was deliberately designed for different tasks which require patience, resilience, multi-tasking capabilities, and many other assets that she would need to cope with the onerous assignment of child-bearing and raising, and managing the home front while still contributing to the household economy.

❖ God gave Adam dominion over all His creations including his helper, but if He had thought that Adam could cope effectively, creation of Eve would not have been necessary. A good team is never made up of members with similar competence and instincts, and the last thing you want in marriage is another you. Unfortunately couples spend a lot of useful time and energy trying to re-mould their partners in their own image. Two magnets of the same polarity repel each other and compatibility means compatible opposites. Couples who are duplicates are boring, self-centered, bringing nothing new, exciting or innovative to the relationship. Marriage becomes great when couples can develop a partnership with shared family responsibilities, help to nurture each other's virtues and assets, adjust to and accommodate each other's deficiencies. Selfishness (I, me and myself) has no place in a great marriage.

❖ God appointed the husband as the head of the wife, "*even as Christ is the head of the church.*" However, headship does not imply authoritarianism (governance without the option of a second opinion or questioning). Leadership by competence and example commands respect and compliance. Headship is not so much authority expressed as a chain of commands as it is an acceptance of a vital chain of responsibilities. The husband should in fact see himself as the family captain pilot and seek to help his wife evolve as a 'co-pilot' who is equally competent to co-lead the family whenever the need arises. Your partner's opinion and advice can be an invaluable game-changer, both of you should develop a capacity to listen to and accommodate each other's opinion and advice. In fact, as your relationship matures, you will find that neither would do anything against the advice of the other.

❖ *"A man (and woman) shall leave his/her father and mother, and cleave to each other, and the two will become one flesh."* This biblical injunction (contemporary translation) is very powerful and loaded, especially when taken together with another biblical instruction: *"Therefore, what God has joined together, let no one separate."* That a couple should continue to honor, respect and support their respective parents and family as long as they live is vital, but they must **both leave home** and cut the existing apron strings, in particular, obstructive, obtrusive interference from relations, and tie new ones with each other. Inability to do this effectively is a potent marriage breaker.

❖ Communication is perhaps the strongest indicator of a successful marriage. Some couples can't stop talking to each other, while others are simply co-habiting and hardly exchange words even when they are alone together at home. Pure communication is not by word only but spirit to spirit and there comes a time when couples can correctly guess each other's opinion on issues. Many issues arise in the family (financial, parenting, conflicts, disagreements, career, etc.) that require intensive dialogue between partners, (not domineering myalogue) to resolve, and couples should strive to develop and sharpen their communication instincts. Quite often, one is an extrovert while the other is a recluse (which is mutually complimentary, being similar would be a problem), and both need to work together to develop a happy medium.

❖ Conflict is healthy, it promotes connection. There will be plenty of disagreements throughout marital life, often starting from day one and persisting to the mature stages of a healthy marriage. Lack of conflict can in fact be symptomatic of disconnection and may mean that couples have given up on each other. However, how conflicts are dealt with and resolved is crucial, starting with a "no winner, no looser" concept. Couples who choose to fight to finish hardly ever finish the fight. Both partners should fight for connection, not knockout. Avoid fight-flight-freeze behaviors and let issues go to rest. Set "red lines" which both of you will always endeavor not to cross, like quarreling in front of the children, resorting to use of abusive, insulting, caustic words or physical combat, or engaging in endless (fire-for-fire) arguments. Name your marital bed 'the Center for Truth and Reconciliation', and vow not to sleep without resolving the issues and conflicts of the day.

❖ When couples take their marital vows, they are not just gaining a spouse; they are inheriting two families as well, and they need wisdom and God's guidance to establish healthy in-law relationships. While stories abound worldwide about intrusive and overbearing in-laws, they could be very valuable assets that should be nurtured, considering the support they give to busy modern working couples especially in child minding all over the world. However, when relationships are potentially toxic, a good strategy is to control and moderate interaction.

❖ Money is often demonized as the root of all evil. However, money is not the problem, it is the *love of money*. Money that is sufficient and available when required to meet the needs of a family is crucial for stability and longevity of a marriage, but relatively few couples manage to make enough to meet even the basic needs (not wants) of the family, and those who make enough have varying concepts about ownership and distribution. This makes money a major stressor in marital relationships. Added to this is the very common need for both partners to meet extended family obligations, particularly in the developing world. The problem is easier when couples work together and pool family resources. Have a healthy discussion as a couple and put in place a financial arrangement that you are both comfortable with. *"Two are always better than one, because they pull together and have a good reward for their labor. For if they fall, one will lift up his fellow.*" If you pull together, you will be surprised to see a third force that pulls you both beyond your imaginations and expectations. It is vital also that couples learn to distinguish between 'needs' and 'wants' and develop a culture of *margin* (disciplined saving culture) to prepare them for the unexpected and the last phase of their lives when lack of adequate funds can lead to premature death.

❖ All men and women are created equal, and there is no room for inferiority or superiority complex in marriage. Relationship in a modern, happy, sustainable marriage should be one of duet/complementation, not duel/competition, it should be a partnership in which assets (wisdom, intellect, compassion, endurance, tolerance, forgiveness, etc.) are fully integrated and shared, since neither of you is likely to have all these virtues. Couples who bond well in partnership are fond of using the word "We" rather than "I, me, myself." Couples should work to set solid, realistic goals, complete with achievement strategies, because a goal without a plan is a wish. Cultivating and nurturing good family values at the early stages of marriage sets a good environment for raising children who are well prepared to face their future with confidence.

❖ The modern wife has graduated from 'helper' to co-provider in addition to her God-given primary responsibility for child-bearing, and the family dynamics need to respond adequately to this new reality. She needs understanding and support from her partner, from childcare through selfcare to homecare. The era of house-help is gone for good, replaced by do-it-yourself and shared-responsibilities, and parents need to sensitize their sons and daughters (some daughters raised in up-scale environment know little about cooking or housekeeping because the family had help) from the early stages of their upbringing on this emerging paradigm shift. Both of them will need good housekeeping and multicare skills in later life.

❖ Many couples are so busy trying to meet immediate family and personal needs that they make little or no provision for the last years when they can no longer work: insufficient retirement benefits, high medical bills could become major stressors in later life. The era of support by children is gone: they have more than enough issues of their own. Couples should start early to prepare for the last lap by working together as one to ensure access to adequate financial resources in their last years, and pray for spiritual guidance.

❖ The life span of marriage is in three phases: most couples spend the first ten years getting to know each other, adjusting to or accommodating differences; they are establishing their careers, and learning to transform from husband and wife to dad and mum. The next twenty years present different issues and challenges: couples start to learn about parenting in real time, and to integrate the challenges with the intensive demands of growing career profiles, from managing infants and toddlers to moderating the independence of teenagers. It is a steep, complex and challenging learning curve and, by the time they have mastered it all, they find they no longer need the expertise because the children have left home !!. This marks the beginning of the third phase: all children have left home and couples are back to 'square two,' with new and equally challenging issues. While the potential for marriage break-up is highest in the first two phases, there is no room for complacency in the final phase: expect new issues and challenges and draw on your wealth of experience to deal with them. Try to develop a conducive, relaxing home environment and common interests that will engage both physically and intellectually. You will also derive a lot of pleasure supporting your married children and bonding with your beautiful grandchildren.

❖ Many new couples think marriage is a bliss and their love boat will be smooth sailing. This is never true, and the misconception leads to frustration which causes them to abandon the ship at the first sign of rough weather. Your spouse, no matter how wonderful he/she may seem during courtship, is not perfect, neither are you. Unless couples develop the strategy of addressing problems, not the imperfections of their spouses, a marriage is likely to fail eventually, irrespective of longevity. People who marry too early or too late are often more prone to divorce because young lovers know little about the realities of life beyond courtship, while older new couples are already set in their ways and accommodation/adjustment becomes difficult.

❖ Marriage breakup has very complex and far-reaching consequences which most couples do not anticipate or comprehend until it is too late. Many issues can lead up to the collapse of a marriage, notably, inability to develop and nurture good partnership qualities; lack of mutual consideration, respect and empathy, selfishness; self-centeredness; financial problems; external interference; and infidelity. Also, the rising economic empowerment of women is giving them greater confidence to walk away from an unhappy marriage. Furthermore, while most men want educated, emancipated, economically empowered women as wives, many have a problem accepting that a co-provider is also a co-authority in the family. Families in some developed countries are already adjusting to this new reality and some even decide that whoever has the higher earning power goes out to work while the other takes care of home.

❖ Divorce is painful and expensive, and the only winners are the divorce lawyers. Neither the husband nor the wife is fully equipped for parenting and the effect of divorce on children is always traumatic, manifesting in several areas of their future life. It is true that there is always an option out there for both of you but you never know the contents of your new baggage until it is too late. There is absolutely no guarantee that a second marriage will work for either of you. It is not surprising therefore that a second marriage has around 50% higher chance of failure than first marriages. Reparation (doing everything possible to save your marriage) should be the first and last option: when the grass is greener on the other side, it is time to wet yours.

Marriage & Inspirational Quotes

"I don't want to be married just to be married. I can't think of anything lonelier than spending the rest of my life with someone I can't talk to, or worse, someone I can't be silent with."
— Mary Ann Shaffer

"You can measure the happiness of a marriage by the number of scars that each partner carries on their tongues, earned from years of biting back angry words." — Elizabeth Gilbert

"It takes three to make love, not two: you, your spouse, and God. Without God people only succeed in bringing out the worst in one another. Lovers who have nothing else to do but love each other soon find there is nothing else. Without a central loyalty life is unfinished." — Fulton J. Sheen

"An archaeologist is the best husband a woman can have. The older she gets, the more interested he is in her."
— Agatha Christie

"A great marriage is not when the 'perfect couple' comes together. It is when an imperfect couple learns to enjoy their differences." — Dave Meurer

"Humility is not thinking less of yourself, it's thinking of yourself less." – C. S. Lewis

"If anything is worse than the addiction money brings, it is the emptiness it leaves". – Derek Kidner

"No man is good enough to govern any woman without her consent". -
— Susan B. Anthony

"Keep your eyes wide open before marriage, half shut afterwards". - Benjamin Franklin

"In a happy marriage it is the wife who provides the climate, the husband the landscape". — Gerald Brenan

"I cant change the direction of the wind, but I can adjust my sails to always reach my destination". — Jimmy Dean

"I love being married. It's so great to find that one special person you want to annoy for the rest of your life". - Rita Rudner

"After 45 years of marriage, when I have an argument with my wife, if we don't agree, we do what she wants. But, when we agree, we do what I want!" — Jacques Pepi

*"Love, the quest; marriage, the conquest; divorce, the inquest".
— Helen Rowland*

"There is nothing nobler or more admirable than when two people who see eye to eye, keep house as man and wife, confounding their enemies and delighting their friends". — Homer

"A successful marriage requires falling in love many times, always with the same person". — Mignon McLaughlin

"Happy is the man who finds a true friend, and far happier is he who finds that true friend in his wife". — Franz Schubert

"My most brilliant achievement was my ability to be able to persuade my wife to marry me". — Winston Churchill

"Neither man nor woman is perfect or complete without the other. Thus, no marriage or family, no ward or stake is likely to reach its full potential until husbands and wives, mothers and fathers, men and women work together in unity of purpose, respecting and relying upon each other's strengths". — Sheri L. Dew

"Nothing in this world can take the place of persistence. Talent will not: nothing is more common than unsuccessful men with talent. Genius will not; unrewarded genius is almost a proverb. Education will not: the world is full of educated derelicts. Persistence and determination alone are omnipotent". — Calvin Coolidge

"The only thing necessary for the triumph of evil is for good men to do nothing." — Edmund Burke

"Men always want to be a woman's first love - women like to be a man's last romance". — Oscar Wilde

"It is not a lack of love but lack of friendship, that makes unhappy marriages." — Friedrich Nietzsche

"To keep your marriage brimming, with love in the loving cup, whenever you're wrong, admit it; whenever you're right, shut up". — Ogden Nash

"Political promises are much like marriage vows. They are made at the beginning of the relationship between candidate and voter, but are quickly forgotten". — Dick Gregory

"Remember that creating a successful marriage is like farming: you have to start over again every morning". — H. Jackson Brown, Jr.

"There is no more lovely, friendly or charming relationship, communion or company than a good marriage". — Martin Luther

"Marriage is an exclusive union between one man and one woman, publicly sealed and physically consummated." — Selwyn Hughes

"Wedlock is a padlock". — John Ray

"Two pure souls fused into one by an impassioned love - friends counselors - a mutual support and inspiration to each other amid life's struggle, must know the highest human happiness; this is marriage; and this is the only cornerstone of an enduring home". — Elizabeth Cady Stanton

"There is nothing noble about being superior to your fellowmen. True nobility lies in being superior to your former self". - -
— Ernest Hemingway

"You know it's never fifty-fifty in a marriage. It's always seventy-thirty, or sixty-forty. Someone falls in love first. Someone puts someone else up on a pedestal. Someone works very hard to keep things rolling smoothly; someone else sails along for the ride." — Jodi Picoult, Mercy

"No woman wants to be in submission to a man who isn't in submission to God!" — T D Jakes

"To say that one waits a lifetime for his soulmate to come around is a paradox. People eventually get sick of waiting, take a chance on someone, and by the art of commitment become soulmates, which takes a lifetime to perfect." — Criss Jami

"Marriage is like God leading you to the Jordan; through faith and perseverance, He will create a way to cross it; the promised land is on the other side." — Afonja

"Blessing always comes with burden. When you are blessed, those who hate you without cause will be too many to count, and too futile to try and counter. Let God do it for you." — Afonja

"Marriage has a way of changing you: your spouse is never the same you courted. The secret of success lies in learning to love and cherish this new stranger." — Afonja

"By all means marry; if you get a good wife, you'll become happy; if you get a bad one, you'll become a philosopher." — Socrates

"When two people are under the influence of the most violent, most insane, most delusive, and most transient of passions, they are required to swear that they will remain in that excited, abnormal, and exhausting condition continuously until death do them part." — George Bernard Shaw.

"To be loved but not known is comforting but superficial. To be known and not loved is our greatest fear. But to be fully known and truly loved is, well, a lot like being loved by God. It is what we need more than anything. It liberates us from pretense, humbles us out of our self-righteousness, and fortifies us for any difficulty life can throw at us." — Timothy Keller.

"The only way love can last a lifetime is if it's unconditional. The truth is this: love is not determined by the one being loved but rather by the one choosing to love." — Stephen Kendrick.

"Marriage has the power to set the course of your life as a whole. If your marriage is strong, even if all the circumstances in your life around you are filled with trouble and weakness, it won't matter. You will be able to move out into the world in strength." — Timothy Keller

"A good marriage is between two forgivers."
— *Ruth Bell Graham*

"Have a good and godly marriage that shows the world Christ's love through how you sacrificially love and serve one another."
— *John Stange*

"Christian marriage is marked by discipline and self-denial. Christianity does not therefore depreciate marriage, it sanctifies it."
— *Dietrich Bonhoeffer*

" As God by creation made two to one, so again by marriage He made one of two." — *Thomas Adams*

"A good marriage isn't something you find, it's something you make."
— *Gary L. Thomas*

"In Christian marriage, love is not an option. It is a duty."
— *R. C. Sproul*

"To make a marriage work, the big three are: Change. Forgiveness. Surrendering to God and being filled with the Holy Spirit."
— *Richard Massafra*

"More marriages might survive if the partners realized that sometimes the better comes after the worse."
— *Doug Larson*

"Scripture says, in all labor there is profit, and nowhere is this more true than in the marriage relationship."
— *Wayne A. Mack*

"What greater thing is there for two human souls, than to feel that they are joined for life–to strength each other in all labor, to rest on each other in all sorrow, to minister to each other in silent unspeakable memories at the moment of the last parting?"
— *George Eliot.*

"There is no remedy for love but to love more."
— *Henry David Thoreau*

"Love recognizes no barriers. It jumps hurdles, leaps fences, penetrates walls to arrive at its destination full of hope."

— Maya Angelou

1 Marriage is a Divine institution

1.1 INTRODUCTION

The definition of marriage depends on the perspective of the writer. Therefore, its meaning varies from one writer to another, from one culture to another, between religious groups and through historical periods. Most definitions project marriage as a universal social institution varying in descriptions of its composition, celebration, process and functionality. In standard social anthropological literature, marriage is defined as a socially or ritually recognized union between spouses that establishes rights and obligations between those spouses, as well as between them and any resulting biological or adopted children and affinity (in-laws and other family members through marriage). God instituted marriage as stated in Genesis 2:15-24: *[15] The LORD God took the man and put him in the Garden of Eden to work it and take care of it. [16] And the LORD God commanded the man, "You are free to eat from any tree in the garden; [17] but you must not eat from the tree of the knowledge of good and evil, for when you eat from it you will certainly die." [18] The LORD God said, "It is not good for the man to be alone. I will make a helper suitable for him." [19] Now the LORD God had formed out of the ground all the wild animals and all the birds in the sky. He brought them to the man to see what he would name them; and whatever the man called each living creature, that was its name. [20] So the man gave names to all the livestock, the birds in the sky and all the wild animals. But for Adam no suitable helper was found. [21] So the LORD God caused the man to fall into a deep sleep; and while he was sleeping, he took one of the man's ribs and then closed up the place with flesh. [22] Then the LORD God made a woman from the rib He had taken out of the man, and He brought her to the man. [23] The man said, "This is now bone of my bones and flesh of my flesh; she shall be called 'woman,' for she was taken out of man." [24] "That is why a man leaves his father and mother and is united to his wife, and they become one flesh". (Genesis 2:15-24).*

The bible passage quoted above emphasizes five Divine guidelines about marriage:

- Marriage was made by Divine order as part of God's extension of His love to mankind. It is part of the grand design to teach us how to love Him, love each other, procreate and populate the world, organize economic production, political structures and social relationships. Before instituting marriage, He provided a location and made provisions for material objects required for survival.

- God created one woman for Adam, implying one man, one wife.

- Man and woman were created to operate as one, the man from the dust of the earth and the woman from bone taken from the ribs of the man. But they were purposefully made differently and assigned different duties. Both bore the semblance of God and were in a state of perfection which implies that one is not superior to the other. Bearing the semblance of God demands respect and humility before God and one another, hence Adam was satisfied with the woman.

- That a man and his wife shall become one flesh implies that the union is indivisible and indissoluble.

- The fifth guideline is clear from the 24th verse of Genesis 2 and is repeated in the New Testament: *leaving father and mother and cleaving to each other is the foundation of the Covenant with God ....and what God has put together, let no one put asunder.* In other words, there shall be no interference from any source whatsoever. The unit is expected to be independent of other units and operate a lifetime commitment model. The implication is that divorce is not permitted. Our Lord Jesus Christ affirmed this vision of marriage when he replied the Pharisees, *"Haven't you read that at the beginning the Creator made them male and female, and said, for this reason a man will leave his father and mother and be united to his wife, and the two will become one flesh"? So, they are no longer two, but one flesh. Therefore, what God has joined together, let no one separate" (Matthew 19: 4-6), a* clear admonition on divorce, reinforced by Apostle Paul in his exposition on marriage: *"Therefore, a man shall leave his father and mother and hold fast to his wife, and the two shall become one flesh" (Ephesians 5:31-32).* In *1 Corinthians 7:10,* Paul admonished *"To the married I give this command (not I but the Lord): A wife must not separate from her husband. If she does, she must be reconciled to her husband. And a husband must not divorce his wife".*

It is clear from the above concepts which derive from Divine instructions that God did not indicate in anyway that one partner is superior to the other (*they shall become one flesh*), rather they were designed to complement each other and compensate for the deficiencies of one another. Patriarchal values predominate in many cultures, with the wife portrayed as an inferior and dispensable 'glorified slave'. This has become a major issue in many modern marriages and a significant source of conflict. Christians must recognize and highlight this biblical *state of perfection and unity* visually, in their imaginations and thought processes notwithstanding the difference imposed by the environment and patriarchal values in most cultures. This is why contemporary writers conclude that *marriage is the uniting of elements that are fundamentally, naturally and beautifully different* and couples must aspire for this mysterious *state of unity* from the beginning to the end.

In a sermon, *"Celebrating the Difference between Men and Women" (youtube.com)*, Adrian Rogers affirmed the unity of marriage by concluding that neither man nor woman is superior to the other but God made men differently from women in order to make them one and for one to complement the other. Adam liked the woman because she was different from the animals and was like him *"flesh of my flesh"*. God created one woman intentionally, not two, a strong indication that He did not approve of polygamy. In respect of these attributes, one writer states that *in marriage the different elements of male and female unite in a complementary, creative and purposeful way* (Dalrymple, 2011). Other writers who have analyzed the difference between the dust and bone/flesh have highlighted its significance in the achievement of synergy in marriage: man as provider versus woman as nurturer; durability of woman versus man's energy; the woman as the romantic versus man as the mechanic, and woman's brain as a radar in contrast to a man's brain as a computer.

The differences in materials and the formation of their brains explain why men and women process information differently. Women use both hemispheres of the brain in dealing with emotion, love and intuition, they are empathetic, they engage in spider-web thinking and detailed explanation of issues. In contrast, men use the left side tuned to logic, reasoning, analysis, calculus, action, with less detail compared with women. These natural differences are required to promote synergy, sustain any union and challenge the notion that being male/female are mere cultural constructs.

Adrian Rogers further explained that the natural bond and creative complementarity of male and female as taught by the Christian Church is rooted in the created order. Marriage is a *social contract* (a Covenant between two people), and is not a *social construct*. He concluded that *"marriage is an enduring social arrangement (an institution) ordained by God, rooted in the different ways in which God has created us, and intended by God as a sacrament of His grace. We are not free to redefine marriage any more than we are free to redefine the laws of physics. We might call something else marriage, but that will not make it so"*.

We should not be oblivious of the many ways in which we have departed from God's instructions, starting with the fall of man in the Garden of Eden, an experience that signified man's departure from the Divine instructions and the evolution of dysfunctional relationships with God and fellow human beings. Contrary to the Divine plan in which there were three partners in the triangular relationship involving God, the man and the woman, the serpent entered as a fourth party and isolated the human spirit from God's Spirit. Satan established a plethora of lies about manhood and womanhood which contradicted God's instructions and corrupted God's concept of marriage. In subsequent Chapters of the Old Testament, there are records of polygamy, homosexuality and in some cultures polyandry etc. Since these non-Christian forms are backed by strong patriarchal cultures and allowed by the legal systems, couples enter their marriages without understanding the meaning and purpose of marriage and without the desired commitment. The good news is that by sending His Son Jesus Christ to redeem us from sin, Our Lord God took us back to the original Divine state thus making it possible for Christians to have *Heaven on Earth* in their marriages.

In most cultures around the world, marriage is a natural progression into adulthood; it marks the beginning of independence and evolution of an identity distinct from one's parents and family members. The majority of adults will get married at some point in their lifespan. However, even with long courtship, the realities of marriage only become evident when couples start to cohabit and most people go into marriage with *fairy tale* expectations. This explains why frustrations and disappointments tend to creep into relationships quite quickly. While there is grave concern worldwide that the institution of marriage is under severe threat and gradually becoming simply one of a number of lifestyle options such as advanced education, career achievement and less formal relationship structures (Mackay 1997), the reality is that it is still the most important goal of the average youngster and society is generally unkind to the unmarried adult.

1.2   MARRIAGE IS GOOD

Marriage is good for many reasons, notably:

- The Lord God declared that it is not good for man to be alone. Therefore, marriage is for companionship. There is a consensus among Christian and non-Christian writers that a spouse is one of the greatest tools that God will ever use to shape mankind, and one of the great vessels of God's grace into your life.
- Marriage is a context through which God expresses His love.
- Marriage is a medium for sanctification.
- Marriage is a medium through which husbands and wives express and share love.
- In marriage, the male is complemented and enriched, edified and humbled, challenged and improved by the female, just as the female is by the male.
- Marriage is for mutual refuge and protection.
- Marriage is an avenue for bringing new life into the world (procreation).

- Marriage is one of the sublime mysteries of Christian doctrine that a relational (Triune), self-giving (sacrificial) Creator God invites his children through relationship and through their self-giving to participate in His constant task of creating and preserving, nurturing and maturing new life.

Although there are many successful marriages around, the failed ones tend to make the headlines, and this is a potent source of uncertainty for new couples who often start off with significant expectations of failure. This is probably one of the main reasons for the increasing divorce rates in many cultures around the world, exacerbated by the negative impact of the increasingly tempestuous modern social life. It is not unusual for friends and family and even Christian counselors to catalogue and overstate the woes to expect in marriage. While it is desirable for couples to be sensitized to these, it is equally desirable to spread the good news that God declared marriage to be good from the onset, and that there are many more successful Christian marriages than failed ones. One writer advises that couples should *"Think of your marriage as an acorn which gets planted on your wedding day. Thereafter, (with good nurturing) it begins to sprout and push up bravely through the dark soil, proudly displaying a few leaves. Slowly but surely as the weeks, months and years pass, the little oak shoot becomes a sapling which grows stronger and stronger. Eventually one day you realize that your acorn has become a sturdy and shady tree, giving shelter and pleasure, not only to yourselves but also to others. So, in simple words the meaning of marriage is to accept the other person and adjust to the various situations that you encounter in marriage to make it really work"* (Marriage.com, 2017).

God made marriage and it was good, so a marriage has a hundred percent chance of success at the beginning. However, growing the relationship from good to great on a foundation that lasts a lifetime, with richly rewarding blessings is hard work and a major test of perseverance. The marital vows are a Covenant signed and sealed in the presence of your God, and should be the guiding light for a new couple on the journey through the unpredictable territories and terrains of life. However, there are many variables that work together to ensure a successful marriage and there is no universally acceptable definition of a successful marriage. Longevity is certainly not a measure of success, otherwise there should be no divorces after decades of marriage; many long-lived couples literally tolerate each other but still live together like strangers, pretty on the outside, broken on the inside. The precariousness of the relationship becomes evident and accentuated when the children have left home. In some cultures, a marriage that is not consummated or blessed with children or a male child, or cannot be controlled by extended relations is a failed marriage. In spite of all these, there is a lot that a couple can do to establish a good marriage, strong and resilient enough to proceed from good to great, built to last.

The lifespan of marriage is in three phases: most couples spend the first ten years getting to know each other and adjusting to or accommodating differences; they are establishing their careers, and learning to transform from husband and wife to dad and mum. The next twenty years present different issues and equally formidable challenges: couples start to learn about parenting in real time, and to integrate the challenges with the intensive demands of growing career profiles. In the third phase, children have left home and couples are back to 'square two,' with new and equally challenging issues. While the potential for marriage break-up is highest in the first two phases, it is not uncommon for relationships to disintegrate after forty something years of marriage unless couples make spirited efforts in the first two phases to grow intense friendship, partnership, mutual love, empathy, and interests that will sustain a close relationship in this final phase.

1.3 THE PENTACORES (FIVE CORES) FOR A SUCCESSFUL MARRIAGE

Marriages are made in heaven, so is thunder and lightning, and couples should expect plenty of both through life in their effort to build a successful marriage. The road to well of happy and successful marriage passes through well of conflict and trial, well of argument, well of persecution, well of opposition, well of temptation, well of obstacles (Biblical David's wells). There is no template for a successful marriage, but there are core biblical guidelines that can help a couple design and build one. Virtually all the pitfalls in marriage are traceable to one or more contraventions of these cores:

- So God created mankind in his own image; in his own image God created them; He created them male and female................Then the LORD God said, *"It is not good that the man should be alone; I will make him a helper fit for him."*

- Then the Lord God made a woman from the rib He had taken out of the man, and He brought her to the man. The man said, *"This is now bone of my bones and flesh of my flesh; she shall be called 'woman' for she was taken out of man. That is why a man shall leave his father and his mother and hold fast to his wife, and they shall become one flesh".*

- *For from Him and through Him and to Him are all things. To Him be glory forever.*

- *Wives submit to your own husbands, as to the Lord. For the husband is the head of the wife even as Christ is the head of the church, his body, and is himself its Savior. Now as the church submits to Christ, so also wives should submit in everything to their husbands. Husbands, love your wives, as Christ loved the church and gave himself up for her, that He might sanctify her, having cleansed her by the washing of water with the word, so that He might present the church to Himself in splendor, without spot or wrinkle or any such thing, that she might be holy and without blemish. In the same way husbands should love their wives as their own bodies. He who loves his wife loves himself. For no one ever hated his own flesh, but nourishes and cherishes it, just as Christ does the church, ... Nevertheless, neither is man independent of woman, nor woman independent of man in the Lord. For a woman came from man, even so man also comes through woman............Let marriage be held in honor among all, and let the marriage bed be undefiled, for God will judge the sexually immoral and adulterous".*

- *"I, ___, take thee, ___, to be my wedded husband/wife, to have and to hold, from this day forward, for better, for worse, for richer, for poorer, in sickness and in health, to love and to cherish, till death do us part, according to God's holy ordinance; and thereto I pledge thee my faith [or] pledge myself to you."*

God made man in His own image, therefore man shall strive at all times to emulate the qualities of God as outlined by Christ and many prophets. God made woman directly from a bone taken from man, a symbol of physical and emotional unity. God gave man a helper, (not helpers), and said that man and woman, (not women), shall leave their fathers and mothers and shall become one flesh. This debunks the common views that God never forbade polygamy. It is interesting to note that God did not mould woman from clay but from bone. While clay structures are strong under certain conditions, the qualities of bone structures are multi-dimensional: clearly she was designed for a different purpose which requires resilience and multi-tasking capabilities. It does not mean in any way that woman is inferior or superior to man, just pleasantly different. Also, no sane person hates his own flesh but nourishes and cherishes it, an implied doctrine (instruction) that man should care for woman selflessly, like his own flesh.

The word 'helper' has been translated into many languages, including 'slave', 'subordinate', 'helpers', 'wives', and there are many potential biblical passages (taken out of context) to choose from in justifying each falsification of God's intention: for example, God already gave man *"total dominion over the fish of the sea and over the birds of the heavens and over the livestock and over all the earth and over every creeping thing that creeps on the earth",* but that was before He created woman. If He had thought that man could cope, creation of a woman would not have been necessary. Furthermore, God stated specific duties assigned to woman which men could not possibly do, like carrying a pregnancy for nine months.

The traditional concepts of marriage which are still prevalent in many traditional cultures can be justified in many ways: man was given full responsibility of providing for and protecting the family, therefore he needed more hands (helpers) who would be directly under his control. This explains the root of polygamy and the need to have many children, especially because life expectancy was unpredictable and largely short. However, in the words of Apostle Paul, *"therefore, if anyone is in Christ, he is a new creation. The old has passed away; behold, the new has come."* Same is very true of marriage. The institution has evolved through all the changing scenes of life to become "partnership." A woman is no longer a helper but a co-provider in many ways, in addition to the onerous God-given assignment of child bearing and rearing. However, this does not in anyway detract from the God-assigned primary duty of the man as the head of the family.

The word 'submit' as used by Apostle Paul has become a potent weapon for men to justify their demand for total submission by their wives. However, reading the biblical passage further shows that Paul gave men the same advice and responsibility, be it in different words. In any case, man does not need to 'demand' submission: any submission received by demand is insincere submission devoid of commitment. By sheer leadership qualities (known as leadership by competence in management theory) a man commands respect from his wife who would hardly do anything that is not approved by her husband. Incidentally, as marital relationship becomes older and more mature, man also would hardly do anything against his wife's advice. This is true partnership and submission to each other.

The word 'God' means different things to different people, depending on their faith. For a Christian couple the belief that *'through God and to God are all things, to Him be glory forever'* is fundamental, thus, making God (through Christ) the cornerstone on which a solid foundation is laid a prerequisite for a successful marriage (all other ground is sinking sand). It is vital that this commitment is mutual and made from the beginning of a marital union, before children start to arrive, so that a tradition that helps them imbibe Christian values seamlessly and without force is already in place.

Every couple takes (or recites) marital vows irrespective of religion, creed or faith - Christian, Jewish, Moslem, Buddhist, agnostic, atheist, capitalist, communist - as a Covenant, and there are significant commonalities: most demand faithfulness and mutual support for better for worse. The bible has strong words and specified consequences for the adulterer; a couple that is not committed to sticking together through thick and thin, through all the joys, trials and tribulations, through all the changing scenes of life that await them, has planted a potent landmine for the relationship. The marriage institution has evolved to the point that some new couples now sign prenuptial agreements, in anticipation and preparation for failure even before the 'examination' has started, yet they take the vows. Where is the faith or commitment?

2 Choice of partner, dating and courtship

2.1 INTRODUCTION

Courtship was the traditional process of selecting life partners for sons and daughters, and the practice varied widely depending on culture, religion and social norms. In many cultures, it was primarily the prerogative of parents to search for the right family to connect with, but a man could also initiate action through his parents if he found a young woman he was interested in. Negotiations were often concluded many years in advance and courtship, regarded as a prelude to marriage was a strictly family affair, with the two families getting to know each other and interacting socially. All meetings between the two young people up until close to marriage were under adult supervision, although parents in the lower social classes may allow the man to take out his fiancee to social engagements, restaurants, movies, etc. There were strict values about physical contact and intimacy. Traditional matchmaking is still common in many traditional cultures and it is not uncommon for a girl under ten years old to be betrothed.

Dating is a modern concept in which two people are attracted to each other, decide to become friends, and start seeing each other frequently, often with the intent of nurturing a close relationship that grows into courtship and eventually leads to marriage. Initially, the permission of the girl's parents was required. However, over time, dating has become flirtatious, largely the prerogative of the two persons involved, and moral values are lax or non-existent. Most young people start dating in their teens whereas the average age at marriage has been increasing over time, which implies that the average youngster may have gone through many dating relationships before eventually settling into courtship. Young people in dating relationships tend to be guided by emotions, they think they are in love but in actual fact, it is infatuation which may grow into enduring love or fall apart.

Modern parents have little or no say in the choice of a dating partner and in fact may not even be aware of the relationship. The dating experience can move the relationship either way: 'for keeps or for kicks.' When both have seen in each other 'something good enough to stimulate a mutual desire for a lasting relationship, it is the beginning of courtship. There is a body of opinion that most men date for fun for a relatively long time compared with women and are not ready for serious relationships. When they feel that they are ready, (and this is getting increasingly delayed into their thirties or even forties) they often settle for whoever they are dating, often not the best in their dating experience. On the other hand women (and their families) start to worry if they are not in a courtship in their late twenties.

2.2   MODERN DATING AND COURTSHIP

The difference between dating and courtship is becoming increasingly blurred, although dating is more informal, not necessarily exclusive and may involve as few as one or two outings; they may just be having fun with no specific expectations; the relationship is often casual and either partner may be dating someone else concurrently. Courtship connotes a more serious and enduring relationship which may eventually lead to engagement and marriage; it is exclusive and monogamous. Not all courtships end in marriage, largely because, as interactions become more intimate, either partner has an opportunity to assess the other and may realize that the relationship would not work. Furthermore, either partner may not really be ready for marriage but may have been responding to his/her flirtatious instincts or societal pressure and obligations. Most couples start dating as friends and either partner has the prerogative to change friends as often as they wish. If they stay together long enough, they begin to show mutual empathy and care more about the welfare and progress of each other. Courtship could last for weeks, or for years, but while longevity is good, it does not guarantee a successful marriage.

Dating is superficial and in the subconscious, and courtship is swimming in the shallow waters of delight; the reality begins when you start to co-habit. Also, it could be hard to spot potential flaws in each other during courtship because both of you strive to be at your best and both of you are wearing rose-tinted glasses which to some extent obscure your vision. However, many potential 'marriage breaker' traits are often obvious during courtship but largely ignored or excused, like short temper, meanness, selfishness, self-centeredness, egoism, flirtatiousness. If your partner shows traits of any of these, it is more constructive, proactive and pragmatic to assess your capability for developing coping mechanisms than to hope for a change. It is easy to fall in love with the virtues of your partner but, can you deal with the obvious flaws which will inevitably become prominent issues in marriage?

The way your friend handles his/her personal stressful situations or yours could be an important indicator of how compatible you might be with him or her. Two emotional hermits who withdraw to their shells will likely have serious marital problems when confronted with tougher issues. People aren't always a mirror image of their family and friends but, in general, you can tell a lot about a person from the kind of friends that he/she keeps, and where they come from. Courtship should be a period of 'getting to know you'; assessing the capacity to cope with the liabilities of each other; ironing out rough edges; seeking wise counsel, and holding joint and individual intensive prayers for

Divine guidance.

In some cultures, match-making is the total responsibility of the elders of the family, mostly the parents who carry out extensive research before choosing a life partner for their child (male or female). Their research areas include family history (including reputation in society, criminal history, hereditary health issues). The intention is good and, although outdated in many modern societies, it is still widely practiced in strongly traditional societies. Unfortunately, the prime focus of the search today by the bride's parents is the socio-economic status of the groom's family. The word "wedding" implies the security the groom's family is capable of providing to the family of the bride, hence future partners are chosen on the basis of their economic worth. Parents of girls usually look out for potential suitors and offer to give their daughters in marriage to the most prosperous suitor, even if she becomes number five or is young enough to be his daughter. This is unfortunate because the new bride is little more that an easily dispensable acquisition, a mere addition to the husband's extended family, subject to all the rules and regulations. Also, the groom's family members believe that they can dissolve the union at will. Recently, a well-educated couple (both medical doctors) from a culture in which arranged marriages are normal, became dissatisfied with the poor relationship of their daughter-in-law with the husband's extended family; they traveled thousands of miles to the developed country where the couple lives, with one mission: to forcibly eject her and terminate the marriage, in spite of their son's opposition. Unfortunately (or fortunately), they spent the night in jail.

It is also becoming a common practice for young women to prefer or even target "men of means." For them, it is no longer wise to marry your equal and commit yourself to a lifelong struggle to make ends meet. Also, the increasingly common paradigm among some women is that a fraction of a large loaf could turn out much better that a small whole loaf: an excuse and justification for walking into a polygamous relationship. Of course such a relationship is devoid of any commitment.

The traditional definition of courtship is the intimate relationship between a male and a female which could lead to marriage. It usually involves spending a lot of time together and attending social and religious functions together. This does not include cohabiting and, in fact, the Christian doctrine forbids sexual intimacy before marriage. However, it is not unusual in modern societies for couples to live together for years or even decades before deciding to get married. In fact, it is quite common in some cultures for off-springs of the relationship to play active roles in the marriage ceremony.

2.3 CHRISTIAN COURTSHIP

Neither dating nor courtship is mentioned specifically in the bible, although there are a large number of resources addressing related issues: love, marriage, immorality, etc. Courtship evolved over centuries as a traditional matchmaking process in which a young male and female interact and get to know each other with a view to developing intimate relationship that could eventually lead to marriage. The primary goal is to find a marriage rather than a social partner. Practices vary widely across cultures: in some cultures, it is the prerogative of the male to find and actively court (woo) a female, and do all he can to enhance her receptiveness to a marriage proposal, and families may or may not be involved at the initial stages. In other cultures, courtship is a highly structured process, with very specific formal rules. Parents and community members may do the matchmaking or hire professional matchmakers who will do the search, evaluation of resumes, short-listing, initial screening, arrangement of meeting between potential partners, and, ultimately the two families if partners and families agree. There are strict rules about the conduct of partners during courtship: they are never allowed to be alone together without an adult chaperon, no option of experimental or serial courtship, no physical contact, close involvement of both families at all stages from the beginning to marriage, etc. Over time, this concept has evolved as the core of Christian courtship, although with different modifications. Also, variants of the process are still practiced in many traditional cultures.

Traditional/Christian courtship is about open and honest exploration of each other's lives and families leading up to engagement and marriage; it is a period of acquaintanceship to know each other as much as possible - personality, family background, past life, ambition, career goals, values, temperament, commitment to the Christian faith, etc. Courtship is a period of togetherness doing things together: praying, worshiping, fellowshiping to seek knowledge from the Bible, Christian literature about marriage and family life, God's counsel and principles on marriage, marital roles and responsibilities, the numerous potential challenges, and Christian warfare in marriage. It is about courting to see if there is any reason why a couple should not get married and it can benefit significantly from the support of vital family, social, and Christian networks. Mandatory adult supervision has become obsolete and most courting couples consider themselves mature and responsible enough to manage their emotions and maintain Covenantal relationship prior to marriage.

Courtship allows for effective communication and agreement about money, discipline, faith, mutual submission and support, helping each other to overcome shortcomings, resolving disagreements, type of wedding, where to live after wedding, church to attend, raising a family, etc. It is a period to give and receive, test compatibility, adjust and adapt to each other socially, emotionally, professionally, academically, getting to know each other's family, sharing things/gifts with each other and families. Courtship enables identification with each other publicly and an opportunity to test-drive your ability to treat each other with respect both in private and as you relate to family and friends. Ideally, courtship once initiated should eventually end in marriage but it is not unusual that partners find themselves incompatible and terminate the relationship. Christian doctrine also promotes courtship between two believers since this greatly simplifies compatibility in terms of faith, spirituality, values, etc. However, when mutual attraction is sufficiently strong, a non-Christian partner will eventually convert to the Christian faith. It should be noted also that there are many Christians happily married to non-Christians but, in most cases, the children are raised to embrace the Christian faith.

Dating is a relatively new concept which evolved in the early part of the last century, largely as a result of rebellion by the youth against the highly restrictive traditional courting process. Furthermore, both males and females are maturing faster because of quality care and are delaying marriage because of educational aspirations which often promote male-female interactions outside the sphere of supervision of their parents. This makes it difficult to suppress the desire of young people to have relationships. In the traditional dating process, two young people of opposite sex do the primary work of finding each other and growing an initially platonic relationship. As they get to know each other and want to start going out on social dates, parents become involved, often regulating the dating process. The traditional dating process was largely chaste since pre-marital sex was not considered the norm, and often led to serious courtship. However, times have changed and dating has become highly flirtatious, casual, experimental, and not mutually exclusive in the last five decades or so. Most young people of today go through many serial or parallel dating experiences before they eventually settle for serious relationships.

In general, literature on dating and courtship treat both concepts as different and mutually exclusive whereas they should in fact be complementary. In spite of the virtues of the traditional courtship process, it is ridden with faults, especially because the two who are going to live together for the rest of their lives often have so little say in the selection process. Also, supervised and monitored courtship means that both partners strive to be at their best, which offers inadequate opportunity for personality assessment on either side. This may explain why strictly traditional courtship is not an insurance for a happy or divorce-proof marriage. A young couple needs to find each other physically attractive to start dating and just one date may be enough to show either that goals are similar and stimulate the desire to grow a genuine, sustainable relationship. The greatest issue with dating is that either or both persons are only looking for a social relationship and pleasure and, considering that dating is now very common among teens, fun is uppermost in their minds.

Children are leaving home earlier than usual, many in their teens, going to college or the world of employment, and may not even be under the influence of their parents. Peer pressure becomes real and, strengthened by sudden freedom; many get into flirtatious and often hurtful dating relationships and sexual activities. Nevertheless, dating could be beneficial because each failed relationship is an experience that can help youngsters avoid similar mistakes in future. Unfortunately, many irresponsible dating experiences end up in unwanted pregnancies, truncated careers, damaged personalities, and even death. Quite often, the dating pair engages in what Bailey (2019) terms 'worldly dating'; they may or may not be on the same page: both may be flirtatious or one may simply be looking for fun while the other is shopping for a life partner. This explains why many dating experiences are fleeting, loaded with lots of intimacy but little or no commitment, often ending in a lot of hurts, heart breaks and scars. In many cases, it leads to unplanned and potentially disastrous consequences which distract young adults from their primary responsibility of preparing for the future, with many ending up as dysfunctional adults and social misfits.

The consequences of unserious dating can also resonate later in marital relationships since fleeting dating could develop a self-centered, feeling-oriented concept of love which teaches people to break off relationships when confronted with the slightest difficulties, conditioning them more for divorce than marriage. Also, a marital partner who has experienced flirtatious dating may develop an appetite for variety and change, creating dissatisfaction within marriage. Increasingly, young people, especially men are delaying marriage to mid/late thirties or even early forties to give themselves enough time to enjoy varied relationships. Such people hardly ever end up in a happy marriage because they are already deeply entrenched in their values and outlook, most of which are incompatible with nurturing happy and sustainable marital relationships. Generally, women are looking for serious relationships by their mid-twenties but many are frustrated by uncommitted male partners who are simply looking for fun and often move on to new relationships.

Dating can be beneficial when both partners are mature and have strong Christian and moral rooting, impacted largely from home, and can discern between right and wrong. Through dating, both can explore each other socially, spiritually, in terms of values and goals, all of which would help determine compatibility for the future. While they may not be able to abide by the ultra-strict Christian Pentecostal rules some of which forbid holding hands, they know the limits which exclude sexual activities in spite of the fact that they spend a lot of time together alone. Usually they get involved in many relationship-strengthening activities such as attending social and religious functions together, jointly working on their spiritual standing, getting to know each other's assets and weaknesses, etc. In many circumstances parents may not even know about the relationship until they have made up their minds to proceed to courtship. In summary, responsible and mature dating could be a very useful prelude to the steep learning curve of courtship. Furthermore, either partner has the opportunity to back out of a potentially toxic relationship before it goes too far and parents become involved. Dating and courtship are vital stages on the route to a happy and lasting marriage because they help in building a solid foundation for a successful marriage. Choosing to ignore obvious 'red flags' in courtship inevitably leads to a miserable marriage: better to have a broken courtship than a broken marriage. It is God's design that every one should have a happy marriage, but this depends on who you date or court and how sensitive you are to obvious signals that could become issues in marriage. To every cause there is an effect, and for every cause there is an effect. If at the courtship stage you notice in your partner any traits that may become an issue in later life, take it up with him/her: a discussion may give you an opportunity to decide whether or not it is an issue that can be overcome or that you can cope with but, above all, go to the Lord in prayers for direction.

2.4   CHOOSING A LIFE PARTNER

One of the most potent causes of marriage collapse is the choice of the wrong partner in the first instance. Factors that could influence the choice of a life partner include the readiness of both partners for marriage, the age of either or both partners and the role of families. There is no template for making the right choice but there are a number of useful guidelines that help minimize mistakes,

2.4.1   Does pedigree matter?

Pedigree is often given a lot of weight in the selection of a spouse: what is the social standing of the family of your partner in your cultural setting? It is not about wealth but about the reputation and respect they command. Although not always, vices and virtues often run in the family. As exemplified in a recent article by Fox Butterfield (2018), crime could be a family affair: "when kids choose a profession, they tend to follow in their parents' footsteps: Doctors' children often become doctors, lawyers produce lawyers, and plumbers beget plumbers". This is of course not valid across cultures. In fact, many professionals come from lowly backgrounds, largely because their parents strive to give them opportunities they never had.

Some families are respected for their Christian values, achievements and positive contributions to society while others are noted for their notoriety. Butterfield quoted studies and statistics in some developed countries which show that crime can run in families: the study followed crimes involving boys over a period of about fifty years and found that half of the convicted kids were accounted for by 6% of all families, while two-thirds came from 10% of the families. Another study found that two-thirds of boys in one area who had been sent to correctional facilities had a father who had been arrested and 45% had a mother who had been arrested. In one extreme case, 60 members of an extended family had been incarcerated or convicted. There is no guarantee that a product of a good home will make a good home or vice versa, but it is useful to know what you are opting for.

Opinions differ about whether or not pedigree matters: while the majority would pass it off as not being important and even discriminatory, a substantial number believes it should be taken into consideration at some point during courtship or dating. While the individuals concerned may not pay attention to it, families and friends would often search to ensure that the family is of right standing in the society. There are of course Biblical examples such as the search for a wife for Isaac, Moses in Jethro's household and Jacob in the household of Laban. In modern society, pedigree would be determined by a host of factors including education, values, wealth, chivalry, class, political stature but also issues of character.

The importance of pedigree varies between people and societies: some people look for future partners who are of similar social status while others want people of higher or lower status. In many societies, women marry men who are of higher pedigree (hypergamy), and often much older largely because future security is of paramount importance. In some cultures, particularly in Asia and Africa, the choice of a life partner is the prerogative of the family, and the consent of either partner is not a prerequisite (arranged/forced marriage). While either or both partners may be unhappy about the match, culture requires that they consent (submit is probably more appropriate) to the marriage. In fact, in some cultures, children are betrothed before they are ten years old.

Regardless of the content of pedigree and the fact that it leverages the base for the couple, it cannot stand alone as a determinant of marital choice. In fact many marriages between persons of similar pedigree do fail, largely because similar pedigree does not imply similar values. In any case, the input of parents in the choice of a life partner is rapidly becoming insignificant particularly in the developed world where partners are being recruited on line, and pedigree is often low on the check-off lists of dating couples. Also, the fact that marriage is becoming increasingly delayed due to increasing priority given to the development of career goals means courting couples are becoming much more mature and independent, and may not involve their families until they need their support at the marriage ceremony.

2.4.2   Right age for marriage

Another important question is the right age to get married. Sixty years ago, age 16 - 21 years would be considered right. However, relatively few people spent more than twelve years on education (many had no education) and marriages were relatively stable because roles were well defined: the husband was the breadwinner while the wife held the home front. Times have changed: both males and females now spend more time acquiring education and career goals. Those who spend less time tend to marry early and the chances of successful and enduring marriages are relatively low among those who get married before the age of 23-27 years. They are more likely to face formidable challenges and stressors including financial, and issues arising from the responsibilities of starting a family at a relatively early age. Those who delay marriage to acquire good education and career prospects tend to be more stable, mature, prosperous, and can better handle the challenges of marriage. However, delaying marriage to early-to-late thirties means that both partners are already stable in their individual careers and having to change habits and values to accommodate a partner may become difficult. In spite of this, there are also advantages: both partners are likely well-educated, mature, goal-oriented, and well set on lucrative career paths with good earning power, which tends to reduce family financial stress significantly. They have also gained useful experience in managing problems and stresses compared with younger couples. A survey was carried out recently among married couples in the United States on age at marriage and the desire for termination, the results are presented in Table 2.1. Only 5-6% of couples in the mature category would consider leaving the relationship compared with nearly 40% of those who married between the age of 20 and 24 years.

Table 2.1 Age of marriage of those who want it to end. *(divorcestatistics.info).*

Age at marriage (Yrs)	Women (%)	Men (%)
Under 20	27.6	11.7
21-24	36.6	38.8
25 - 29	16.4	22.3
30 - 34	8.5	11.6
35 - 39	5.1	6.5

2.4.3   Risk factors

In a book: "Ten Important Findings on Marriage and Choosing a Partner - Helpful Facts for Young Adults", Popenoe and Whitehead (2004) provide basic guidance; a list of values, backgrounds, interests, and goals that indicate a greater likelihood of a successful marriage as listed below:

- An introduction by family, friends, or acquaintances (that is, a member of a social network) is the most effective way of bringing together individuals of similar values, backgrounds, and interests.

- Men and women who are college educated are more likely to marry, and less likely to divorce, than persons with less education.

- Unwed women who become mothers have a lesser chance of marriage than childless women.

- Marriage as a teenager is the highest known risk factor for divorce. People who marry in their teens are two to three times more likely to divorce than people who marry in their twenties or older. Also, people who leave it late, say to their mid-thirties are likely to find adjustment and accommodation difficult because they are already set in their ways.

- Serial cohabitation, particularly before the first marriage, increases the probability of both marital discord and divorce.

- Married persons are more likely to have emotionally and physically satisfying sex lives than single persons or cohabitants.

- Marriage enhances one's income and wealth. As a general rule, married persons achieve greater income and wealth than cohabitants.

- Persons who are the children of divorced parents are slightly less likely to marry, and when they do marry are much more likely to divorce.

- Even though the divorce rate in America remains steady at 50%, it is significantly less than 50 percent for educated persons in a first marriage; persons who are 25 or older at the time of first marriage; when neither partner has cohabited with several partners before marriage; and when both are strongly religious, especially when they are of the same religion.

Despite the romantic notion that people meet and fall in love through chance or fate, the evidence suggests that social networks are important in bringing together individuals of similar interests and backgrounds, especially when it comes to selecting a marriage partner. The results of many studies have shown that married partners introduced by family members, friends, co-workers or other acquaintances have the highest chance of successful marriage compared with other sources. This is probably because whoever is doing the matching already knows a lot that is positive about either or both partners, that could enhance compatibility. The more similar people are in their values, backgrounds and life goals, the more likely they are to have a successful marriage. Opposites may attract but they may not live together harmoniously as married couples if they are unable to make the necessary adjustments. People who share common backgrounds and similar social networks are better suited as marriage partners than people who are very different in their backgrounds and networks.

Women have a significantly better chance of marrying if they do not become single parents before marrying. Having a child out of wedlock reduces the chances of ever marrying or staying happily married. Despite the growing numbers of potential marriage partners with children, one study noted, "having children is still one of the least desirable characteristics a potential marriage partner can possess." The only partner characteristic men and women rank as even less desirable than having children is the inability to hold a steady job. Evidence from many studies in the United States suggests that education is a positive factor in marriage: Both women and men who are college educated are more likely to marry, and less likely to divorce, than people with lower levels of education. Despite occasional stories in the news predicting lifelong singlehood for college-educated women, these predictions have proven false. Although the first generation of college educated women (those who earned baccalaureate degrees in the 1920s) married less frequently than their less well-educated peers, the reverse is true today: college educated women's chances of marrying are better than less well-educated women. However, the growing gender gap in college education may make it more difficult for college women to find similarly well-educated men in the future. This is already a problem for African-American female college graduates, who greatly outnumber African-American male college graduates. Furthermore, living and sharing power with an educated woman is a new (and often steep) learning curve for men, and this explains why the earliest educated women had difficulty in getting married.

Trial marriage (living together before marriage) reduces the chances of a successful marriage. People who have multiple cohabiting relationships before marriage are more likely to experience marital conflict, marital unhappiness and eventual divorce than people who do not cohabit before marriage. People are likely to be less discerning in selecting partners they co-habit with, there are no set goals and aspirations beyond daily co-existence, and they are likely to form core habits in an informal environment which may become detrimental to a happy marital relationship in later life. People who grow up in a family broken by divorce are slightly less likely to marry, and much more likely to divorce when they do marry. According to one study the divorce risk nearly triples if one marries someone who also comes from a broken home. However, the increased risk is much lower if the marital partner is someone who grew up in a happy, intact family.

The discussion above highlights the multi-dimensional nature of potential pitfalls in the selection of a life partner. It is vital therefore to use the period of courtship to look for traits and factors which may facilitate and promote compatibility, or become issues in marriage, notably:

- Physical, sexual and intellectual attraction.
- Shared values (about faith, social life, career goals, money, nuclear family structure, extended family relations).
- Past history of your partner.
- Mutual respect and consideration for each other.
- Honesty and reliability.
- Constructive communication.
- Genuine interest in each other's life, goals and aspirations and commitment to joint planning.
- Spirit of forgiveness.
- Spirit of consensus as opposed to authoritarianism.
- Supportive instincts.
- A good sense of humor.
- Anger management.

2.5 GETTING TO KNOW YOU: REALLY?

Ideally, a good courtship is a fine opportunity to get to know each other and guarantee marital bliss. But the question is does it? There is no doubt that time is needed for a relationship to mature, hence couples should avoid rushing to the altar. The dating and courtship process should establish deep friendship, love and commitment for the day to day operations and when problems arise. The tests come unexpectedly: when deciding where to live after marriage, career issues, daily routines and division of labor in the home, management of family wealth, number of children to have, when and how to space them, parenting style, the friendship network, the church to attend and relationships with in-laws etc. Resolving each of these issues requires drawing on one or more of the above attributes to reach a consensus. Couples should not hesitate to seek counseling if necessary, in any case many Christian churches insist on pre-marital counseling. Each partner should seek to know the best attributes of the other, as well as the not-so-good attributes - it is overoptimistic to expect a drastic change in your partner after marriage, hence you need to know what you can live with, possibly for the rest of your life. It is important to get to know the family of your partner, they will inevitably play a significant role in supporting (or disrupting) your marriage. Unfortunately, many courting couples are too involved in the romantic aspects of dating and often miss, ignore or condone obvious red flags.

2.6   PRAYING AS A DATING COUPLE

Dating is for the purpose of getting to know each other and discerning whether or not you want to stay together for life and, quite often, you may not want to stay together. Spiritual connection is important for a dating couple but individual spirituality is even more vital. You need to go to your God in prayers for guidance in looking for the right signs and the wisdom to discern between acting and reality; to distinguish between infatuation and genuine attraction. A Christian dating partner does not necessarily turn out to be a Christian spouse. You also need to pray for your partner that God navigates you both to the same page spiritually, and helps you know if your partner's faith is genuine. If both of you accept God as Number One in your individual life, then He needs to be part of your relationship from the start. Maintain your own personal relationship and prayer life with God and put Him first in your life. *"Above all else, guard your heart, for everything you do flows from it"* *(Proverbs, 4:23)*, not just your body until the wedding day. One writer says that, too often we prematurely give our hearts away to people and wonder why our life feels like a storm, or we feel deeply hurt when we are let down. Relying on any other person as your foundation or anchor can expose you to *dependence syndrome.* Identify common interests that can help your joint spiritual growth, like attending seminars and bible classes, reading books by experienced Christian authors, holding spirited discussions about the cardinal points of faith. Some experts have suggested that praying together can also be very useful because spiritual life already becomes a regular part of your relationship, and this helps you to establish flow patterns of behavior and relationship over time, and implanting devotional and prayer in your relationship as a married couple would be seamless. Praying together can help purify your relationship as it grows since neither of you would like to do something wrong under the watch of your Creator.

However, it is important to note that prayer is a deeply intimate relationship with your Creator and you always feel free to reveal all your weaknesses to Him and seek help. You need your own one-to-one time with God to be completely real and forthcoming with your thoughts, feelings, insecurities and dreams without worrying about who else is listening. Both of you should focus on being personally strong spiritually, then you can complement each other if and when you eventually come together as husband and wife. It should be noted also that, by praying together, you could inadvertently give your partner a bit too much of yourself, which can be exploited. A partner whose spirituality is peripheral can put on an act if he/she knows it is a sure way of winning you over. If things don't work out eventually, you can feel a deep sense of exposure and rejection. In any case, it is far more important to concentrate on sharpening your personal relationship with God, and praying together should be complementary, and, better still, you can jointly identify prayer points that you both want to put before God in your individual prayers. By all means, share all the things you have learned and that God has revealed to you personally and choose appropriate sections of the bible for in-depth discussion. Gradually, each will notice and assess the other's spiritual commitment, and what to expect in later life together.

3 The marriage ceremony

3.1 INTRODUCTION

The marriage ceremony is a very important part of marital life": it is the process by which two people make their relationship public, official and permanent; when they take their vows before their God and living witnesses; it should be as memorable as possible. The marriage ceremony is an elaborate affair in virtually all cultures, religions, and social strata, and for good reason: traditionally the woman is being given a befitting sendoff for a daughter who is leaving home, and this explains why her family does most of the spending. This tradition is in contrast with the biblical decree that *man and woman shall both leave their homes and become one*, and gives the husband's family members a good reason to regard a wife as 'new acquisition'. It is also largely responsible for the very common problem that arises from them because they regard their son's house as an extension of theirs and his wife an addition to the family hierarchy. It is not uncommon even in modern cultures for the mother of the groom to compete with the bride for prime attention in marriage ceremonies. In many traditional cultures, the ceremony ends with the handover of the bride by her parents to a delegation of the groom's family. Although the practice of treating the bride as an addition to the groom's extended family whose name she must acquire is cross-cultural, it is becoming less of a problem in developed countries. In fact, it is increasingly common for brides to retain their own family names. However, it is still a prominent marriage breaker in the developing world because it provides easy justification for the very common interference in the marriage by the groom's family.

3.2 THE MARRIAGE CEREMONY

The marriage ceremony should be as grand as possible, and the marriage industry is booming all over the world, driven largely by the power of the media. Traditions vary across cultures, with different stages of activities, notably introduction (families meet formally for the first time), engagement, bride shower, wedding ceremony, and honeymoon. In many traditional cultures, the marriage ceremony is a reflection of the social and financial standing of the bride's family and ceremonies could last just a few hours or extend to as long as two weeks. Most couples plan meticulously to ensure a successful and memorable ceremony, and it is now a norm to engage the services of professional planners. In some traditional cultures, much of the expenditure is on expensive jewelry and bride price, and the bride's family bears the brunt. However, in modern cultures, the couple is primarily responsible for the expenses of marriage.

Virtually every country in the world has traditional rituals which must be performed by the couple to ensure good luck in the relationship and keep evil spirits away from the marriage, varying from the bride wearing something old, something new, something borrowed, something blue, to weird and often repulsive practices, like the bride's father spitting on her before she leaves for her husband's home. For example, in France, the couple must eat chocolate and drink champagne after the reception - from a toilet bowl; in Sweden, guests are allowed to kiss the bride or groom if for any reason the spouse leaves the reception hall; in Hindu culture, the bride must first marry a tree; Congolese bride and groom are forbidden to smile on their wedding day, from ceremony to reception in order not to give the impression that they are not taking the ceremony seriously. The German bride and groom take their first test in partnership immediately after the ceremony: they must jointly clean up piles of used dishes and rubbish thrown around their home by friends to ward off any evil spirits. The couple is also presented with a large log of wood and a saw, they must saw the log in half as a team to prove their ability to work together as partners in overcoming obstacles in their marriage. The Greeks have a tradition of having the groom's face shaved by his best man after which his new mother-in-law feeds him with honey and almonds. The Japanese traditional ceremony is particularly interesting: as part of the ceremonies, the bride must wear a hood which symbolically hides the "horns of jealousy" she feels towards her mother-in-law. In Indonesia, newly wedded couples are confined to their home on special diet for three days during which they are not allowed to use the bathroom or empty their bowels. This is believed to strengthen their bond. In the morning of the wedding, a Russian groom must go to the home of the bride's parents to pay a 'ransom' or present gifts to his future in-laws, dancing and singing. After the wedding, the couple takes turns to bite a specially baked bread without using their hands, and whoever takes the biggest bite is considered the head of the family. In a Chinese culture, the bride must shed tears (of joy) for one hour a day, starting one month in advance of the marriage ceremony; her mother joins her after ten days, grandmother and other females in the family also join every subsequent ten days.

Over time, marriage has become a social competition, with couples seeking to outdo previous ceremonies of friends and relations, to the extent that they accumulate debts which eventually become an albatross in the early stages of their marriage, particularly if the couple does not have high income or they already have a financial burden arising from their education. It is a well established fact that wedding-related debt is the source of major conflicts in the early stages of marriage due to inability to provide funds for the most urgent needs of a young couple, particularly in modern cultures in which the couple bears the expenses of marriage. Wisdom and rationalism need to prevail to ensure that the ceremony does not threaten the marriage. It is vital that couples should 'cut their coats according to their cloth (not size).' Many stories abound of conflicts that arise during and immediately after the wedding: choosing the scale of the ceremony, how much to pay, who pays for what, the location, the number and types of guests, and accommodation for guests who cannot pay their hotel bills, especially family members, the honeymoon, etc.

Patrilocal rules of residence often encourage the newly wed to live with parents. In many cases, family members who lived with their sons before the wedding would sometimes continue to stay for long periods of time. This often happens irrespective of class, race and education but such practices are more common in traditional cultures. Even in the developed world, the husband's parents could stay for over six months after the wedding. In some traditional cultures the husband is expected to set up home in the family compound and the wife takes her place in the extended family hierarchy. Also, tradition requires sons to look after their siblings, including their education, and this is extending to married daughters as well. Quite often, they are the most promising in their respective families and feel obliged to help their siblings. This could become a heavy load on the young family's financial stability. In some extreme situations young husbands could be required to fund the education and living expenses of as many as ten siblings and relations.

The most important part of the marriage ceremony that is often underplayed is taking the marriage vows, the Covenant of a couple with each other and with God. It is a solemn vow to commit yourselves to the relationship for life, an expression of faith in and dedication to your marriage in the presence of Almighty God. There are many versions of marital vows and each couple should select one that they are both comfortable with, or modify the wording as desired. For example, many couples decide to replace 'to love and to obey' with 'to love and cherish' and other couples choose to write their wedding vows. This aspect of the ceremony should be taken very seriously because the vows are designed to be in effect "till death do us part" but, unfortunately, they are soon forgotten.

There are also some anachronistic practices in Christian marriage ceremonies that inadvertently encourage the enslavement of women, like the standard ceremonial question: "who giveth this woman away?" The bride's father is required to affirm and physically hand over his daughter. In some modern cultures, the bride's father only accompanies her on a walk down the isle to show approval of the groom. It is not unlikely that even this practice will give way to equal treatment and the bride will walk down the isle with her chief bridesmaid, just like the groom does with his bestman. Another practice in traditional Christian marriage ceremony which has become contentious is asking the bride to "love and obey", which is now giving way to "love and cherish." These changes may sound too radical for some traditional societies but, inevitably, realities will catch up with perceptions, be it at different rates in different societies.

3.3 WHAT'S IN A NAME?

It is the traditional practice that the bride should drop her family name and adopt the husband's last name. In modern times, some women are choosing to retain their family names or adopt compound names, an indication of potential disunity from the start. While this may sound feminist, there may be some justification for the new trend. As discussed earlier, the traditional practice implies that the bride has dropped her identity and integrated fully into the husband's family. This procedure has become largely symbolic in some developed cultures and is not a significant cause of conflict in marriage. However, it could have serious implications in traditional societies.

In some cultures, the family of the wife has to pay heavy dowry to the husband's family as a mark of gratitude for accepting their daughter. The new wife is considered junior in hierarchy to all the children of the extended family and other wives already in the family, irrespective of age. When any member of the extended family has an event, the new wife is expected to relocate temporarily and serve as cook and steward. The wife may lose all rights to own any property in her name, and everything owned by the new couple belongs to the extended family. A sixty something year old man dies and his extended family sends for *all* his belongings, including his wife who they could give away to another member of the family. Also, the extended family can decide on when it is time for their son to disengage from the relationship if they are dissatisfied with his partner, and they arrange for a replacement. These are obnoxious and no longer acceptable to the modern woman, but the practice is still prevalent in many traditional cultures. It also explains why growing family wealth jointly in a marriage can be problematic.

The traditional concepts of marriage often create a major *balancing act* problem for the *modernized* husband who wants to keep his extended family and nuclear family *happy* but *separate*. Having to drop family name implies complete obliteration of the bride's past; on the other hand, the 'new trend' practice where a bride retains her maiden name is an onerous sign she does not intend to leave home. Ideally, and in obedience to God's instruction *"Therefore a man shall leave his father and his mother and hold fast to his wife, and they shall become one flesh",* a new couple should both drop family names and adopt a fresh family name, but we are a long way from this development.

3.4   CHOOSING POST-MARITAL ABODE

In most traditions, the wife moves to the house of the husband. Subsequently they may decide as a couple to find a more convenient home especially when babies start to arrive; they may decide to live close to relatives, or far away from them although, in some cultures, couples have little choice on where to live. Some couples decide to relocate to distant places in order to minimize extended family interference but they miss out on potential family support which could be invaluable in some circumstances. In matrilocal cultures, the husband moves into the house of his wife's mother; in patrilocal cultures, married couples cannot set up an independent household but must be part of an extended family compound.

Marriage is a Covenant between two before God

"Haven't you read that at the beginning the Creator made them male and female, and said, 'For this reason a man will leave his father and mother and be united to his wife, and the two will become one flesh'? So they are no longer two, but one flesh. Therefore what God has joined together, let no one separate."
Mathew 19:4-6

"May your fountain be blessed, and may you rejoice in the wife of your youth. A loving doe, a graceful deer— may her breasts satisfy you always, may you ever be intoxicated with her love". Proverbs 5:18-19

"Two are better than one, because they have a good return for their labor: If either of them falls down, one can help the other up. But pity anyone who falls and has no one to help them up. Also, if two lie down together, they will keep warm. But how can one keep warm alone? Though one may be overpowered, two can defend themselves. A cord of three strands is not quickly broken"
Ecclesiastes 4:9,12

"By wisdom a house is built, and through understanding it is established. Through knowledge its rooms are filled with rare treasure." (Proverbs 24:3-4)

"Love is patient, love is kind. It does not envy, it does not boast, it is not proud. It does not dishonor others, it is not self-seeking, it is not easily angered, it keeps no record of wrongs. Love does not delight in evil but rejoices with the truth. It always protects, always trusts, always hopes, always perseveres. Love never fails. But where there are prophecies, they will cease; where there are tongues, they will be stilled; where there is knowledge, it will pass away. .....And now **these three remain: faith, hope and love. But the greatest of these is love"**
1 Corinthians 13:4-8, 13

"With all humility and gentleness, with patience, bearing with one another in love, eager to maintain the unity of the Spirit in the bond of peace."
Ephesians 4: 2-3

"Do to others as you would have them do to you." Luke 6:31

"Hatred stirs up conflict, but love covers over all wrongs." Proverbs 10:12

"Whoever does not love does not know God, because God is love." 1 John 4:8

"Do not urge me to leave you or to return from following you. For where you go I will go, and where you lodge I will lodge. Your people shall be my people, and your God my God. Where you die I will die, and there will I be buried. May the LORD do so to me and more also if anything but death parts me from you".
Ruth 1:16-17

4 Startup: getting to know each other and building a great marriage on a solid Christian foundation

4.1 INTRODUCTION

Irrespective of the duration and success of courtship, the reality starts when couples start to live together. What was evident but ignored or excused during courtship could become major issues and potential marriage breakers, and new issues which had not been apparent or anticipated will inevitably emerge at different stages of marital life. Factors in the external environment of the home also create surprises just as factors in the home: extended family issues, sudden ill health, job loss, career challenges, etc. Couples need to develop strategies for dealing jointly with all kinds of threats to their relationship and follow them closely.

No matter how long and intimate your courtship or how compatible you are, you will find yourselves at the beginning of a new and steep learning curve. Both of you are imperfect and would have tried to be at your best during courtship. However, the real you emerges when you start to live together. Inevitably, there will be differences, often serious ones but, in the words of Dave Meurer, *"A great marriage is not when the 'perfect couple' comes together. It is when an imperfect couple learns to enjoy their differences"*. The initial stage in marital relationship is a period of mutual adjustment and mutual accommodation, a period when you learn to nurture the assets of your partner and manage the liabilities, when you learn to cultivate mutual respect and empathy, and jointly deal with issues that are inevitable - commitment to your marital vows, dealing with conflict, financial issues, external interference, personal tragedies, etc. It should be remembered that partners process issues differently: the wife is empathetic and accomplished in scoping techniques (fully analytical on precedence, possibilities, probabilities, effects, risks, consequences, sustainability); the husband is mono-directional on objectivity and achievement-orientation. Over time, couples learn to reconcile their differences amicably; they learn to listen to each other without being judgmental; they learn to be less selfish and avoid humiliating each other; they personalize each other's problems; they learn to empathize with each other; they avoid the use of foul language; they learn to control anger and resolve conflicts. How a couple succeeds in coping with the issues of the first five years or so can be a strong indicator of an enduring marriage.

The ten commandments have specified the core values that help build a solid marriage and family foundation *"For no other foundation can anyone lay than that which is Christ."* God created marriage not just as a Covenant between a man and a woman, but rather a man and a woman in a growing relationship with each other and with Him as the third member of the union. The more you love God, the more capacity you will have to love each other. The core of the commandments is '*love*,' a word which has a very wide range of connotations. Love by its nature isn't a fairy tale feeling, but a commitment which has no happy ending: it is a story with no ending. *"Love never gives up, never loses faith, is always hopeful, and endures through every circumstance"*. Genuine love will inspire you to keep all the 'thou shalt nots', from committing fornication and adultery to murder.

4.2   BECOMING ONE FLESH

"A man shall leave his father and mother, and cleave to his wife, and the two

will become one flesh." This is a very powerful and loaded biblical injunction especially when taken together with another injunction: "*Therefore, what God has joined together, let no one separate*". That a couple should continue to honor and respect their parents as long as they live is vital, but they must cut the existing purse and apron strings including obtrusive interference from relations and tie new ones with each other. Inability to do this effectively is a potential marriage breaker. However, this does not absolve a couple of their responsibilities to their extended families, especially their parents.

According to Apostle Paul, "*Two are always better than one, because they pull together and have a good reward for their labor. For if they fall, one will lift up his fellow. But woe to him who is alone when he falls and has not another to lift him up! Again, if two lie together, they keep warm, but how can one keep warm alone? And though a man might prevail against one who is alone, two will withstand him.*" Modern marriage should be a duet/complementation (not a duel/competition); it should be a partnership in which assets (wisdom, intellect, compassion, endurance, tolerance, forgiveness, etc.) are fully integrated, since neither of you is likely to have all these virtues. Couples should work to set solid, realistic goals, complete with achievement strategies, because a goal without a plan is a wish. Couples who bond well in partnership are fond of using the word "we" rather than "I, me and myself."

4.3   THE POWER OF A PRAYING FAMILY

Our day-to-day survival in spite of the numerous potential dangers that surround us is by grace, not by right, and we should have a lot to be thankful for. There is a common saying: "*A family that prays together, stays together*" and this has been supported by recent statistics: 50% of marriages in the United States end in divorce, and 78% of second marriages also end in divorce, but less than 1% of couples who pray together daily end their marriages. Praying together daily as a family does not in anyway replace the development of your personal relationship with God, in fact they complement each other in a very powerful way. Prayer should be the core of a Christian marriage but is often relegated to the background because of the 'rat race' daily schedule of most modern families. Jesus said: *"Again, I tell you that if two of you on earth agree about anything you ask for, it will be done for you by my Father in heaven"* (Matthew. 18:19). Praying as a family enhances marriage in many ways: it nurtures a strong bond between couples and makes it easier to discern God's will and purpose in your marital life; it provides a very rich venue for praying with one accord and for one another; it lays a strong foundation for a spiritual legacy for your children which can be passed on through generations; it promotes mutual understanding and tolerance which in turn minimize conflicts; testimonies abound on the way prayers have helped couples including the authors of this book to surmount difficult and traumatic issues in marriage. Prayers keep you both humble before God, help to sharpen the intimate relationship between one another, and promote mutual understanding, accommodation and adjustment.

Clarence Shuler's in-depth research on how to make your spouse your best friend (2000) identifies eight core benefits of praying with your spouse, which are summarized below:

- Prayer keeps you humbled in front of your God and your spouse.
- Prayer removes you from the cycle of hurting each other.
- Prayer releases your deepest hurts.
- Prayer unites a couple.
- Prayer breeds mutual appreciation.
- Prayer is an invitation to change.
- Prayer removes selfishness.
- Prayer gives a couple hope.

Your personal prayer is a dialogue with God, and when your spouse is involved, it becomes a trialogue, the power of which is aptly expressed in Ecclesiastes 4:12: *"And though a man might prevail against one who is alone, two will withstand him - a threefold cord is not quickly broken"*. Many couples only pray together when there is a troubling issue, or before a meal, or in church. Garrett Higbee (2019) has listed a number of reasons that may account for paucity of family prayers:

- No real prayer life on your own.
- A lack of honest and open communications with your spouse.
- A fear your prayers will be judged or inadequate.
- No margin in your life, so by the time you could you are too tired.
- No role models so you are not even sure what it looks like.
- Your flesh, Satan, and the world's distractions.

God has decreed that couples should come together as one flesh and praying together is like cementing a commitment to marriage, joint spiritual growth, and love for one another. Prayer can be shallow, sporadic and unfocussed, but intimate, desperate, family prayers woven into the rhythm of family routines, addressing personal, career and family issues are powerful. Heart filled prayers together pretty much cements a life-long bond that is not easily broken. Pray together first thing in the morning and last thing at night and allow for one minute of silent prayer when each participant places before God a personal request or wish. Developing a habit of joint prayers embedded into a family routine prepares the grounds for a seamless integration of children into the culture. It is quite common for five-year olds to lead family prayers at the dining table or family prayer sessions. Holding joint family prayers should not preclude continued sharpening of each spouse's personal relationship with God through individual prayers at every opportunity, including while driving to work. It provides the opportunity to seek God's supreme intervention in very personal issues and issues with your spouse, marriage, in-laws that are not appropriate family prayer points.

4.4 COMPATIBILITY IN MARRIAGE

As discussed earlier, God deliberately created man and woman for different purposes, to interact in harmony, complement each other and compensate for the deficiencies of each other. In effect, it is unlikely that a couple will be totally compatible initially. However, there are many basic compatibility issues that should feature prominently in serious dating and courtship: religious/spiritual beliefs and practice, social values, convictions and interests, finances, parenting, role expectations, communications, management of stress and crisis, recreational interests, etc. Significant compatibility on these issues should play a key role in helping either partner to evaluate the other and decide on the wisdom and prospects of such a union. Compatibility does not imply sameness, it means the ability of a married couple to integrate their assets and accommodate their differences, often turning them to an advantage in the best interest of the family. For example, two people who have similar hot temper or are both self-centered have little chance of growing a successful marriage unless they are both predisposed to seeking professional help. A couple is considered compatible when they can merge and grow the assets brought to the relationship by each, and develop synergy in managing or helping to overcome each other's deficiencies.

Learning to deal with deficiencies could be a long and arduous process, often starting with hurt/rejection and progressing through tolerance to accommodation. Along the way, many of the deficiencies often disappear due to growing mutual understanding, adjustment and maturity. In a recent best seller on strengths based marriage, Jimmy Evans and Allan Kelsey (2016) applied the well established strengths-based assessment methodology (that has been successfully used in business evaluation and leadership training) to the institution of marriage, with interesting results. Couples who had been married for a long time were requested to identify and list their strong virtues in order of priority. Jimmy Evans and his wife Karen who had been married for over four decades each listed 34 values. Jimmy's strongest value was 'achievement', which was number 34 on Karen's list. On the other hand, Karen listed 'empathy' (caring) as number one, which was last on Jimmy's list. This scenario often misconstrued as incompatibility is typical of most marriages and is often one of the main causes of friction in the early years. What makes a marriage evolve from good to great is the ability to harness these obvious and significant differences over time in such a way that they complement each other and account for the deficiencies of one another, helping the development of a richer, deeper relationship. Issues that require achievement are best left to Jimmy while Karen applies her multi-dimensional empathy intelligence to connect emotionally with and help other members of the family and beyond.

4.5 ADJUSTMENT AND ACCOMMODATION

Marriage is a very complex institution: most couples believe that getting married and having children is the end of the story, in fact, it is only the beginning of a complex, intricate course of a long-term relationship. Quite often, it is a relationship between two incompatibles as aptly expressed by George Bernard Shaw: *Marriage is an alliance entered into by a man who can't sleep with the window shut, and a woman who can't sleep with the window open.* The course of true love and enduring marital relationships never runs smooth, it is full of ups and downs and twists and turns. Young couples often go into marriage with unrealistic expectations. Your spouse, no matter how wonderful he/she seemed during courtship, is not perfect, but neither are you. Prepare yourself for disagreements, disappointments, adjustments and accommodation, and you will receive less shock on the bumpy road to a happy marriage. A successful marriage is not by chance, it is by change, the ability of both partners to discard unrealistic expectations and move from their 'comfort zone' to a 'unity zone.' *"Through wisdom a house is built and by understanding it is established."* (Proverbs 24:3). Each partner comes to the relationship with a baggage full of virtues, but with a decent mix of vices as well. Quite often, one stands still and expects the other to do all the adjustment. In effect, you are trying to create another you, and, apart from creating a monotonous and boring marital relationship, it could be akin to bringing two positive (or negative) magnets together - they repel each other. Both partners must be committed to change and adjustment to each other in order to grow a mature relationship. In a recent article, Alain De Botton (2017) summarizes seven rules to help move a marriage from good to great and built to last:

- **Expectation of perfection is unrealistic**

  Couples should accept from the outset that both of them and anyone they would come across in their journey through life will be very far from perfect in many deeply serious ways. It is important therefore that, from the onset, couples are aware of the specifics of their imperfections and the potentially negative impact on their partners. Some earlier dating experiences may help to emphasize that no one is perfect and imperfection comes in different shades and colors. In effect, seeking perfection is unrealistic, the goal should be 'good enough'.

- **Be humble enough to accept blame**

  Difficulties will inevitably arise in serious relationships, and the tendency is to blame your partner or someone else, oblivious of the fact that both of you are trying to achieve something at which almost no one succeeds completely - perfection. Rather than strive to adjust ideas and expectations, relationships are terminated in the hope that new relationships will be devoid of the anomalies of the last one. This may be true but different issues will inevitably arise. It is not uncommon for dating partners to eventually settle for a life partner who is significantly more flawed than many of the earlier dates.

- **Eliminate unrealistic and irrational demands of your partner**

Your life partner is expected to be your best friend, closest confidant and first choice for support. However, this is an ideal that soon fizzles out as a result of unrealistic demands of either partner and lack of respect for his/her limitations. Your best friend can quickly transform into a monster to be hated and abused. Selfishness is at the root of this problem: one partner stands still and expects the other to make all the adjustment, offers little or no support while the other is multi-stressed. The job description of a typical modern home is too complex to seed to one partner, especially when both are working: making enough money to meet the basic family needs; household chores, child raring and parenting; health issues, extended family issues, etc. Inevitably, relationships will degenerate quickly and the oppressed partner will eventually seek a solution, often through separation or divorce.

- **Be ready to love rather than be loved**

It is easy to focus more on being loved than loving: your spouse isn't giving enough but are you? As the family grows and children arrive we find that the need to love rather than be loved grows exponentially: the children expect their parents to be spontaneously on hand to comfort, guide, entertain, feed and clear up, while remaining almost always warm and cheerful. Most parents end each day too tired and stressed to complain about inadequate love and wondering if they gave enough.

- **Relationships require administration**

Instinctively, couples tend to focus on the emotional aspects of their marriage whereas a marital home is in fact a small business that requires an effective and innovative system of administration and management: budget planning and administration, allocation of household chores, dealing with unexpected and unanticipated problems, family welfare and safety, managing external affairs and relations. Effective leadership capable of mobilizing, involving and motivating all family members is a prerequisite for growing a successful marital home.

- **Understand that sex and love do, and don't, belong together**

The general view expects that love and sex will be aligned. But in truth, they won't stay so beyond a few months or, at best, one or two years. This is not anyone's fault. Because relationships in the long term have other key concerns (companionship, administration, another generation), sex will likely suffer. We are ready to get into a long-term relationship when we accept a large degree of sexual resignation and the task of sublimation.

- **Effective management of differences**

The right person is expected to be someone who shares our tastes, interests and general attitudes to life. This might be true in the short term. But, over an extended period of time, the relevance of this fades dramatically; differences inevitably emerge, arguments over domestic and relationship issues will emerge. The person who is truly best suited to us is not the person who shares our tastes, but the person who can negotiate differences in taste intelligently and wisely. It is the capacity to tolerate difference that is the true marker of the right person. Compatibility is an achievement of love; it shouldn't be its precondition. The mutual ability to accommodate and manage differences plays a key role in consolidating a resilient marital relationship.

4.6   CONFLICT RESOLUTION

There will be conflicts in marriage, and expect plenty of them, possibly starting from day one, often triggered by disagreement on division of labor and money issues: who cooks the meals, who washes the dishes, who pays for what. The reality is that many 'millennial wives' know little or nothing about cooking or housekeeping (mothers or home help did it all) whereas many men are still traditional, expecting the wife to cook and look after the home. While modern home gadgets have greatly simplified home keeping and pre-packed meals have taken drudgery out of home cooking, no marital relationship is likely to survive for long if the home depends entirely on external assistance (including eating out which should be an occasional family treat), and it would be an unfortunate value to pass on to children. It is not difficult for both wife and husband to pick up the art of home keeping: wives can devote a few hours of each weekend to experimenting with widely available recipes, while husbands keep the home tidy by vacuum-cleaning and helping with the dishes. Husbands can also become excellent cooks if they choose to try (remember that the leading chefs in the world are men !!), and many grow a tradition of preparing Sunday breakfast for the family. Apart from the fact that sharing home-front responsibilities promotes companionship, it can be fun and it helps share the load of modern housekeeping since few families can afford external help.

There will be many other conflicts, both internal and external, and couples need to evolve joint strategies for dealing with them. The baseline is that couples quickly develop mutual respect for each other, communicate positively and constructively, grow the spirit of forgiveness and consensus, and commit to real-time full resolution of conflicts. The reality is that a partner will often back off and the conflict remains unresolved only to resurface, often energized by other issues. Women tend to be more emotional in conflict situations and expect sympathy, while men tend to look for a prompt solution (not necessarily an optimal solution). In a compassionate good-to-great marriage, individual interest (mine versus yours) is sacrificed for collective interest, couples focus on the stability of the relationship and seek to meet the social and emotional needs of one another.

Disagreements nearly always inflict injury (emotional or physical) on either or both partners. The ability to forgive each other is a vital factor in conflict resolution in marriage. However, according to Fincham *et al.* (2004), forgiveness has three dimensions: retaliation, avoidance and benevolence. In younger marriages, either partner (more likely the husband) seeks retaliation while the wife tends to be benevolent (which helps to pacify her partner). Neither strategy helps to resolve conflicts and both may intensify the frequency and seriousness of disagreements. In more mature relationships, both forgiveness models still feature prominently but either partner (usually the husband) may now develop avoidance strategy which seems to resolve issues from his own point of view but, in reality, only delays more conflagratory disagreements in the future.

4.7   MANAGING ANGER AND MALICE

Some liabilities cannot be eliminated, like anger or malice which is a reflex reaction beyond the instant control of the source. However, it is always fleeting and often referred to in psychology as temporary insanity because it hardly ever lasts beyond a few minutes (those who sustain anger for long are sick and need help). Annoyance is natural, but when combined with ego, it becomes anger. Anger is a weakness not a strength as perceived by many who often use it as a weapon to control others; the one who is angry is the first to be set on fire before it impacts on anyone else, hence, both suffer. Bearing the insult and effect of anger is in fact a display of great strength. Anger is an expression of self-righteousness: you believe that your standpoint is right and are intolerant of other views or opinions when you feel insulted, or when you incur a loss. One writer describes anger as a transformation from a human being into a beast, a loss of control of your internal machinery. Ability to remain calm in the face of provocation is one of the greatest assets a human being can have. An angry person deserves sympathy, not confrontation. The inner heat generated by anger is intense, often brief but self-destructive, and this is why remorse often follows quickly.

Anger is a normal, healthy emotion, a problem arises when it cannot be kept under control. Anger is an effect, not a cause and the only way to control anger is to address the cause. Anger can be managed because you can feel it coming, your heart beats faster and you breath more quickly; management is the ability to get out of the situation before you lose control. One psychologist recommends that counting to ten gives you time to cool down so you can think more clearly and overcome the impulse to explode. She also recommends that you try breathing out for longer than you breathe in, and relax as you breathe out: this calms you down effectively and helps you to think more clearly. If you are a Christian, there are short verses in the Books of Psalms and Proverbs (Table 4.1) that one can memorize and repeat several times to help cool down. The spouse of an anger-prone partner needs to develop coping mechanisms (for example, by trying not to confront anger with anger). It will not take long for your angry partner to come down and apologize (or appease if too arrogant and conceited). Anger is often short-lived but extremely dangerous because the consequences can be profound: an angry person can go as far as commit murder in a split moment, only to spend the rest of his/her life dealing with the consequences. Anger is gender neutral, either partner has the potential capacity, and needs the help of the other to manage the syndrome, like one keeping quiet while the other boils and then initiating a conversation to resolve the issue. The anger-prone spouse also can adjust by training self to say little or nothing when angry, possibly by removing self temporarily from the scene.

Table 4.1   Bible passages about anger, malice and forgiveness

The vexation of a fool is known at once, but the prudent ignores an insult (Proverbs 12:16).
Know this, my beloved brothers: let every person be quick to hear, slow to speak, slow to anger; for the anger of man does not produce the righteousness of God (James 1:19-20).
Refrain from anger, and forsake wrath! Fret not yourself; it tends only to evil. For the evildoers shall be cut off, but those who wait for the LORD shall inherit the land (Psalm 37:8-9).
If anyone thinks he is religious and does not bridle his tongue but deceives his heart, this person's religion is worthless (James 1:26).
Be angry and do not sin; do not let the sun go down on your anger, and give no opportunity to the devil (Ephesians 4:26).
Complete my joy by being of the same mind, having the same love, being in full accord and of one mind. Do nothing from rivalry or conceit, but in humility count others more significant than yourselves. Let each of you look not only to his own interests, but also to the interests of others (Philippians 2:2).
Do not say, "I will repay evil"; wait for the LORD, and he will deliver you (Proverbs 20:22).
So put away all malice and all deceit and hypocrisy and envy and all slander (1 Peter 2:1).
In these you too once walked, when you were living in them. But now you must put them all away: anger, wrath, malice, slander, and obscene talk from your mouth (Colossians 3:7-8).
So whatever you wish that others would do to you, do also to them, for this is the Law and the Prophets Mathew 7:12).
A soft answer turns away wrath, but a harsh word stirs up anger Proverbs 15:1).
And whenever you stand praying, forgive, if you have anything against anyone, so that your Father also who is in heaven may forgive you your trespasses (Mark 11:25).
For all have sinned and fall short of the glory of God (Romans 3:23).
What causes quarrels and what causes fights among you? Is it not this, that your passions are at war within you? (James 4:1).

Malice/sulking is a form of anger which is only different in expression. Even though sulking is passive, it can be more deadly than anger because it can last much longer. While an angry husband bullies his wife one minute, then tries to hug her the next minute, a sulking wife can switch off for days, weeks or even months. Nevertheless, this combination is still much better and safer than two with inflammatory anger disposition; it gives the angry person time to reflect and try to make amends. However, a person who keeps malice also needs help, especially because he/she is the main victim of the inner burning and suffering; it has as much potential to destroy a marriage as visible anger. While neither anger nor malice is curable, each person in a marital relationship can help the other in developing management strategies, such as one trying to keep sane and put a temporary stop to the issue while the other is temporarily inflamed by anger, or gently humoring a sulking partner. Furthermore, there are many Christian and psychological resources and counseling facilities on anger management.

4.8   COMMUNICATION

Communication is perhaps the strongest indicator of a successful marriage. Some couples cannot stop talking to each other even at social events, while others are simply co-habiting and hardly exchange words even when they are alone together at home. It is very easy to develop your own selfish comfort zone in a marriage and nurture your interests, often at the expense of your partner's. Pure communication is not by word only but spirit to spirit and there comes a time when one can read the mind of the other with decent precision. Many issues arise in the family (financial, parenting, conflicts, disagreements, career, etc.) that require dialogue (between partners, not domineering myalogue) to resolve, and couples should strive to develop and sharpen their communication skills and instincts. Quite often, one is an extrovert while the other is a recluse, and both need to work together to develop a happy medium. Withdrawal behavior by either partner as a reaction to conflict is very common and can contribute significantly to an unhappy marriage. Also, each partner often thinks the other is the cause of the problem. Couples need to do self-examination and see how their individual behaviors are contributing to a conflict and work together to develop mutually respectful conflict management strategies that do not require a winner or loser.

4.9   LEADERSHIP BY EXAMPLE

Some men cling to Apostle Paul's instruction about wives submitting to their husbands, they should read the passage further to fully appreciate the fact that submission is meant to be mutual. Furthermore, Paul did not intend that a wife is a doormat, on the contrary, the passage was meant to promote verbal, spiritual and emotional intimacy between spouses, and either will have to sacrifice a little bit of 'self.' This does not in any way detract from the husband's God-given authority as the head of the family (which very few women will challenge). However, authority comes with enormous responsibility, and competence in dealing with responsibility translates to effective leadership and authority. *"For the husband is the head of the wife, even as Christ is the head of the church."* Headship does not imply dictatorship; it is not so much authority expressed as a chain of commands as it is an acceptance of a chain of responsibilities.

Wives need to appreciate the fact that a man's ego is in transition. History projects him as a commander-in-chief, with a battalion of several hundred women and children under his command. He was also the sole provider and protector. He still enjoys similar status today in many cultures, but often without the will to accept the responsibilities that go with the position. Imbibing modern marital partnership concepts which implies the sharing of responsibilities is a very common problem. Wives need to appreciate this problem and work to help their partners overcome this 'superiority complex.'

4.10 GENDER ROLES IN MARRIAGE

The biblical instructions about gender roles in marriage are clear from the discussion in the last section: the husband is the head of the household, provider and defender, while the wife is a "help-meet" (a suitable helper), child bearer and "chief of staff" of the home. This arrangement worked very well when life on earth was largely agrarian, and it is still prevalent in many traditional cultures. However, this dynamic has shifted dramatically in the last fifty years or so in response to the changing pattern of employment in the global workforce. It is useful here to examine in some depth the case of United States which to a large extent typifies the trend in other developed cultures, and is gradually infiltrating many traditional cultures in the developing world (see Christian courtship 2019). Manufacturing (regarded as a man's world) which had dominated the industrial world for centuries began to give way to other professions like medical care, home health assistance, childcare, information technology, catering, retail in the last fifty years or so.

The feminist movement gained speed in parallel with the mass entry of women into education and the workforce. With the increasing emergence of automation and more efficient technologies, employment opportunities for men began to recede while opportunities opened up for women who are more suited to many of the new employment opportunities associated with human development. Job opportunities in manufacturing have shrunk by around 50% and one in five men are currently unemployed compared with one in fifteen in 1950. Of the fifteen job categories projected to grow fastest over the next decade, men are likely to dominate only two of them: janitor and computer engineer. As a result of more women entering the workforce, around 70% of children are now growing up in households in which all adults are in the workforce, a potential though surmountable marriage stressor.

One major implication of the paradigm shift in traditional gender roles is its effect on the earning power on women. Currently, nearly 30% of women earn more than their husbands and, considering the exponential rate of increase in the population of women with college and postgraduate degrees, this proportion is bound to keep rising. Men are beginning to come to terms with this rising challenge to their traditional role as provider and many are opting for the role of "help-meet": about 25% of husbands now take on the primary role of running the home while the wife makes more money, compared with only 4% in 1970. However, while this development is progressive, it is a direct challenge of the man's ego and mutual adjustment and accommodation skills are prerequisites for success in marriage. Studies have shown that many men are coming to terms with traditional role reversals but it will take time to surmount the inevitable change in power dynamic between spouses, especially because of societal taboo. Furthermore, men are unlikely to perform household chores to the satisfaction of their wives and this could become a significant source of frustration and tension. Some recent studies have shown that some husbands who find themselves in this situation actually experience feelings of inferiority complex, loss of self esteem, and self respect, sometimes leading to divorce and, to some extent accounting for the exponential increase in the number of single parent households headed by women.

4.11 LAYING A SOLID FOUNDATION FOR A HAPPY MARRIAGE

Marriage can be great if it is structured on the right paradigm, if the two participate fully and have voice, if it is based on clearly defined values, aspirations and goals, if it is a good match, if the right preparations and adjustments are made, if the age is right and if it is not rushed. While it is

external threats. It can be very useful if couples take a day off now and then and get away from routine environment it they can, in order to provide a conducive atmosphere for constant review of progress and consolidation of their relationship.

Experts recommend the triangular theory which defines the components of love and their relationship with marital satisfaction. The higher the positive relationship between intimacy, passion and commitment, the higher the level of marital satisfaction. And the greater the discrepancy among the three components, the lesser the satisfaction in the relationship. Intimacy is defined as closeness and connectedness toward another person which removes psychological boundaries and brings about the desire to share one's innermost thoughts with the other. According to Erickson (2014), the establishment of intimacy is the central task of a young adult wherein one acts considering some or all aspects of the partner thus expecting ones' self-concept an indicator of the level of relationship intimacy. Self-concept is critical to the evaluation process because it assists individuals to assess their self-worth or self-esteem in the relationship, identify one's feelings, needs and the sincerity to share and then facilitate the initial steps towards intimacy with others. Young married partners tend to seek deep intimacy and satisfying relationships. It should be noted that building intimacy involves making sacrifices to be able to trust, care and accept one another. Making sacrifices influences the depth of the relationship, level of satisfaction and the ability to reject poor alternatives to the relationship. It would be impossible to grow a happy, lasting and cast iron marital relationship if either partner is not willing to make sacrifices for the relationship.

Passion is an important component of marital satisfaction. It is described by Tung Tong Pui (2007) as ' intense emotion accompanied by physiological arousal and persistent sexual desire, longing and excitement for each other'. Based on this, couples must be great lovers, must have a volatile relationship and dominate each other's life. As indicated already, this means that couples must spend time together, touch each other, engage in physical intimacy and exhibit strong emotions including jealousy. Both partners should make special effort to develop age-proof strategies that ensure they remain physically and emotionally attractive to each other. According to Barber (2002), Kurup and Kurup (2003) the emotions displayed with concentrated attention, expectation of a reward and a sense of giddiness are chemically fueled by dopamine that changes the chemistry of the brain. Unfortunately, passionate love is variable with individuals, with time and culture and because it could fade rapidly it does threaten the longevity of marital relationships. Endless expectations of bliss sometimes lead to misery, disappointment and disillusionment.

Commitment is the third main component of marital satisfaction, a true mark of intimacy that sustains the relationship through thick and thin. Commitment is developed collectively with trust in the relationship but is usually promoted by feelings needed by one partner. It encourages pro-relationship acts or things that are good for the relationship, builds trust, security and emotional attachment for the couple. Commitment tends to develop in the middle ages from around 35 - 40 years old when career, work and parenting have taken the central stage of family life, and deepen with time. Barber and Kurup concluded that *'couples who are committed to each other work through troubled times and find the quality of the relationship greatly enhanced. Those who have fewer problems express their love for their partners more often, have higher levels of marital satisfaction and are committed to their spouses as persons'*. In effect, marital satisfaction is based on how well expectations match what is being experienced. Scott and Schwartz (2007) offered some gratifying conclusion that despite the increase in divorce and separation, many couples claim to be happily married and would marry their spouses again.

4.12   MANAGING FAMILY WEALTH

Money is often referred to as the root of all evils. However, the problem is not with money but with *love of money*. In fact, optimal access to money is an *essential commodity* in marriage: too little or too much often spells doom for marital relationships. It is vital that couples are able to meet the financial needs of the family but the problem is with the definition of *need* as opposed to *want*. When money is scarce, couples tend to focus on need, but the increasing viral infection of credit offers and aggressive marketing of consumer goods have blurred the distinction between need and want. Gone are the days when people cherished the longevity of their possessions. Couples are encouraged to *spend now and pay later*, a model that helps promote non-essential spending, like changing a functional home, vehicle, furniture, television or cell phone to contemporary models. Love of money drives the desire to acquire more than is necessary to maintain comfortable family life, it promotes desire for even more money (honestly or dishonestly) to fund undesirable instincts and acquire luxury items. However, throughout history, people have become enormously wealthy simply by fully utilizing their God-given talents such as hard work, perseverance and innovativeness. Such people tend to maintain relatively simple lifestyle despite their enormous wealth, and channel most of their wealth to charitable causes.

Tradition recognizes the husband as the primary family provider but coping with the modern family budget is beyond the capacity of the average man. The wife's contribution is becoming increasingly invaluable and, in cultures where polygamy is still practiced, the mother has near-total responsibility for the welfare of her children, including education. The first marriage was blessed with significant resources, the Lord God assessed them and concluded they were good, so did Adam. It was obvious after the fall of man in the garden that the man and woman had to work harder for their human and material resources and the responsibility and ownership had to be shared. The duties of the man and those of the woman were designed to be complementary but, unfortunately, as kingdoms and new civilizations developed, a patriarchal and materialistic culture emerged, the complementary family system changed to a competitive and hierarchical one, with women being subordinate to men. Who owns and manages family resources is therefore one of the major areas of conflict in marriage and family life today.

God designed a power-balance structure for the family: both men and women had their jobs to do and neither is self-sufficient, they needed each other. However, over time, the model of 'men worked and women managed the home front' has conferred men with power because the contribution of women was regarded as unskilled and less valued. This power imbalance has been a primary source of conflict in marriage and, in the event of a divorce, the wife is often left with nothing. Fortunately, in many modern societies, the contributions of partners are placed on equal footing in deciding the sharing of family wealth in the event of a split up. Also, the concept of prenuptial agreement is gaining ground and no longer reserved for the rich.

Over the last few decades family circumstances have changed, families are becoming discrete entities and the family income has to be sufficient to meet the minimum needs. The era of live-in extended family relations or nearby family members who help out in many ways is gone and, increasingly, the husband's earnings are no longer sufficient to meet the bare minimum needs of the family. Fortunately, women are becoming increasingly educated, economically strong, and can contribute significantly to the family purse. However, this requires restructuring of the family power dynamics – from authoritarianism to power sharing. Managing modern family wealth has become a major challenge due largely to lack of trust, and many couples not only operate as individuals, they go to great lengths in hiding resources from each other. It is quite common for a spouse who dies intestate to lose all hidden assets because neither the partner nor anyone else knew of their existence. There is ample research evidence that marriage helps people to generate income and wealth: compared with those who merely live together, people who marry become economically better off. Men become more productive after marriage; they earn nearly half as much as do single men with similar education and job histories. Home front stability; marital social norms that encourage healthy, productive behavior and wealth accumulation; and more efficient specialization and pooling of resources play a vital role. Furthermore, married couples enjoy many social benefits such as tax allowances which enable them have more money to meet family needs. The family finances are even stronger when the wife also works, especially for couples who succeed in evolving financial management strategies which they are both comfortable with.

It is vital that families develop the culture of *margin* from the start: never spend all that you earn. Unfortunately, the opposite is increasingly becoming the norm - most people spend more than they earn, they accumulate debts and often become insolvent eventually. Lack of margin precludes *adequate* provision for retirement (pension schemes never provide enough), or the ability to respond to unexpected emergencies such as loss of job, illness or loss of a loved one. Couples who imbibe the culture of saving often pass it on to their children from an early age and this helps the children aspire to similar models in their adult and marital lives.

While there is no unique template for managing family wealth, there is little doubt that working together as a couple helps grow resources beyond levels achievable by individual efforts. However, there must be mutual trust and couples should work out arrangements that they are both comfortable with. Some old-school couples pool resources to grow family wealth. However, this requires total mutual trust, and is probably not the best option for young couples. A model which seems to work for many couples involves jointly running a family purse to which each contributes a decided proportion of earning and from which family finances such as mortgage payment, utilities, food, children's expenses are met. This leaves room for some financial independence for each partner, for example, meeting extended family obligations of making individual investments in properties, shares, etc. At the same time, individual investments are open and are frequently determined jointly. In the event of a built-to-last marriage, assets are usually pooled to fund the expenses of the last years as married couples, while partners who divorce still have some individual financial assets.

4.13   FAITH AND FINANCE

Mahatma Gandhi once said, *"The fact is, the moment that financial stability is assured, spiritual bankruptcy is also assured."* This statement is clearly a reflection of the words of Christ: *"It's easier for a camel to pass through the eye of a needle than for a rich man to enter heaven" (Mark 10:25).* John Wesley (1789) also said: *"Wherever true Christianity spreads, it must cause diligence and frugality, which, in the natural course of things, must beget riches. And riches naturally beget pride, love of the world, and every temper that is destructive of Christianity".* Karl Marx (1867) *wrote: "Money is the estranged essence of man's work and his existence, and this alien essence dominates him and he worships it".* As discussed earlier, there is nothing wrong with the blessing of riches but, given the way we often manage money and allow it to become our ruler, subsuming our spiritual standing with God, blessings can become curses. Material blessings are eternal and many of us make fortunes by utilizing God-given talents, but it is easy to become distracted by the desire to keep multiplying and storing our wealth here on earth, investing increasing amounts of time and energy in protecting and multiplying the blessings. It is perhaps useful here to reflect on a few extracts from the testimonies of Julian Archer (2013) who belongs to the top percentile of the world in terms of wealth, and who now runs a Christ-focused faith-versus-finance ministry:

- When a person prospers, either God gains a partner or the person loses their soul.

- Somewhere between joining the globe's wealthy in the revered "1% Club," and becoming spiritually bankrupt, Jesus knocked on the door of my heart again. Scrambling over the mountain of blessings that I'd piled up inside my heart, I pulled hard on the door handle, but it wouldn't budge. What now?

- For way too long I got my energy from making profit graphs soar upwards. This had some lovely perks, but it also seriously taxed my relationship with Jesus—not that I dared to admit it at the time as I was still an "active church member".

- When I "build bigger barns" and store up my treasures here on earth, accumulating God's material blessings like real estate, investments and finances, they easily distract me from eternal riches. I start to worry about them, and I invest increasing amounts of time and energy into protecting and multiplying the blessings, instead of trusting completely in Him. My finances rise, but my faith falls—and I often don't even realize it (see Rev. 3:17).

- I have found in my life, the first indicator of spiritual apathy is the cropping of my early morning time with God. This usually occurs during periods of increased time pressures due to financial, personal, entertainment, or other priorities. The problem could last just a few mornings or many years.

- When I neglect to spend quality time praying and studying the Scriptures every morning, my relationship with Christ dwindles.

- Whenever I fill my heart with the gifts instead of the Giver, my faith falls. When Christ knocks on the door of my material-blessings-filled heart (Rev. 3:20), the sound of His knocking is muffled, and even when I do hear it, I struggle to climb over all my blessings to reach out and open the door.

- I desperately, but secretly, wanted to be converted--again--but life's distractions and pressures held me too tightly. God had blessed me with so much--family, career, friends, income, investments, vacations--that I was too busy with the blessings to make time for God. After years of searching, I finally did discover how to reignite my 'first love' with Jesus and now I can't shut up about it!

Financial blessings can easily turn into curses unless properly managed. Evidence abounds that faith and finance are foes: the wealthier we become, the less our faith in the Giver. Statistics show that nations that have been richly blessed have also become poorer in their standing with God. In a survey on wealth versus faith conducted by Gallup across 114 countries in 2009, more than half of those earning $25,000 and above did not consider religion an important part of their daily life, compared with only 5% of those earning $2000 and below (see Table 4.2). When data from this source is combined with country data extracted from Credit Suisse Global Wealth Report (2013) as shown in the lower half of the table, the strong disparity between the rich and poor countries is evident. Clearly, the higher the per-capita income of a nation, the lower the role of religion in their daily lives. It is also significant that seven of the ten richest countries who think that religion is not important in their lives are in Europe where Christianity was nurtured. One of the greatest challenges in life today is how to manage opulent blessings of riches without loving the gift more than the Giver; without being self-centered, self-righteous and arrogant; giving what belongs to the Giver, and sharing the blessings with others who are not so fortunate. A noteworthy development is the Giving Pledge campaign initiated in 2010 by Bill Gates and Warren Buffett, two of the world's richest men. The initiative is designed to inspire the wealthy people of the world to give at least half of their net worth to philanthropy either in their lifetime or upon their death. To date, nearly 200 individuals from 22 countries have pledged around $400 billion.

Table 4.2   Statistics on faith and finance
(Gallup 2011; Credit Suisse 2014).

Gallup question: Is religion an important part of your daily life?		
Median responses by per-capita income, mean adult wealth and country		
Per-capita income ($)	**Yes (%)**	**No (%)**
0 – 2,000	95	5
2,001 – 5,000	92	7
5,000 – 12,500	82	17
12,501 – 25,000	70	28
25,000 +	47	52
Country	**Mean Adult Wealth (US$,000)**	**% Answered "NO"**
Switzerland	513	57
Australia	403	67
Norway	380	78
Luxembourg	315	64
USA	301	36
Sweden	299	88
France	296	74
Singapore	282	53
Belgium	256	68
Denmark	255	83
Thailand	8	2
India	5	9
Haiti	4	8
Pakistan	4	4
Kenya	3	3
Cambodia	3	3
Nepal	2	5

4.14   PREPARING FOR RETIREMENT

Many couples are so busy trying to meet immediate needs that they make little or no provision for unexpected emergencies and for the last years when they can no longer work. While many employers and states have retirement benefit schemes, stipends are never enough to meet the future needs, especially medical care which will inevitably become urgent and expensive. Government-sponsored benefits are constantly being revised downwards in developed countries while in many developing countries entitlements are often not paid for months or even years. Furthermore, many retirement schemes managed by the private sector often collapse, leaving beneficiaries in the cold. It is potentially beneficial if either or both partners are self-employed since there is no mandatory retirement age and children often take over family businesses.

The culture of investing in children so that they can invest in you in later years is becoming increasingly obsolete. Life is getting increasingly tough and demands on the finances of the nuclear family are rising, hence most children struggle to keep afloat (thanks to mortgages and credit cards), and there is little room for parents. It is important therefore that couples start making provision for retirement from an early stage, including taking out reliable life/accident insurance policies, buying stocks and shares of reputable companies, and investing in real estate in potentially commercial locations. Couples can do both individual and joint investments to diversify the base and spread risks.

The consumer world is growing at an exponential rate, reinforced by multiplicity of media and advertising technologies, such that the ability of the individual to distinguish between *need* and *want* is becoming increasingly compromised. The wide availability of credit – credit cards, deferred payments, soft loans, etc. – is tempting many families to live beyond their means, and statistics show that a lot of couples are ending up in penury in their last years. It is vital that couples develop a *saving/margin culture* (spend less than you earn) from the early stages of their marriage, putting aside a specific proportion of their income "for the rainy day" and never touching it except in cases of extreme emergencies. In the words of Warren Buffett: *"Do not save what is left after spending; instead, spend what is left after saving"*. This requires strict budgeting and investment in reliable financial instruments (which reduces temptations to dip into savings). This may be done jointly or individually depending on adopted financial arrangements. However, in spite of separate saving arrangement, couples need to work together in deciding on major investments: "two heads are always better than one". It is also vital to inculcate this discipline in the children at a very early age in managing their allowances.

4.15   SEX IN MARRIAGE

Intimacy in marriage implies both emotional and physical connection between couples, and it is vital that it features prominently in an enduring marital relationship. Sex is a key component of physical intimacy which makes a couple happy; it fulfills a human basic need of closeness and connection; it enhances bonding; it is not limited to intercourse but includes cuddling, oral and manual stimulation and sharing of sexual fantasies. The frequency and quality of sex between couples depend on a lot of factors, including age, values, lifestyle, innate sex drive, health, and most of all, the quality of their relationship. Sex drive can vary significantly between couples: in the words of a psychologist, "even the most compatible couples aren't libido twins" (Jory 2018). Also, there are many external stressors: work stress, health issues, relationship issues, parenting chores, dwindling downtimes, etc. There is no magic number for how often happy couples have sex but a recent study (Twenge *et al.* 2017) on American couples found that people in their 20s have sex 80 times a year on average compared with 20 times in their 60s. Another recent study found that happy couples have sex roughly once a week and found no evidence that more frequent sex made couples any happier while those who had less frequent relationship reported less fulfillment. However, each couple needs to develop their own model, based on mutual satisfaction and spontaneous response to each other even when one is not on the same page in terms of desire. Also, over time, each partner develops strategies for arousing the interest and positive response of his/her partner.

Sexual relationship between couples is usually at its peak in the early years often referred to as the infatuation and discovery phase. Sex drive also decreases with aging and this explains why it often becomes a treat in long marital relationships. Furthermore, there comes a time in your relationship where mutual confidence is well-established, you know nearly everything about each other, and life's stresses and obligations start to be more of a priority; testosterone levels decline in both males and females and sexual drive slows down. This can become a serious issue in marriages that are devoid of close connection or there is a significant mismatch in sexual drive. Life can feel monotonous and boring, and the once virile stimulus may become less enticing. However, among couples who are committed to and on track for an enduring union, sex relationship moves into the 'maintenance phase' but still remains an important part of a long-term marital relationship; it is a vital tool for reconnection and, according to psychologists, brain chemicals released during sex further enhance bonding.

Contrary to popular belief that sex in marriage is boring and infrequent, numerous statistics show that people who are married are more likely to have emotionally and physically satisfying sex lives than single people or those who just live together. Married people report higher levels of sexual satisfaction than both sexually active singles and cohabiting couples, according to the most comprehensive and recent survey of sexuality. Almost half of wives interviewed in a recent study said that they found sex extremely emotionally and physically satisfying, compared with less than a third of single women who had a sex partner. The proportion of husbands who said sex was extremely satisfying emotionally was significantly higher than wives (over half), while only one in three of cohabiting men who expressed satisfaction. The higher level of commitment in marriage is probably the reason for the high level of reported sexual satisfaction: marital commitment contributes to a greater sense of trust and security, less drug and alcohol-infused sex, and more mutual communication between the couple. Medical statistics also show that married couples who have sex regularly live longer, have better heart health, enjoy a deeper connection, and are less prone to anger and malice. Also, body chemicals released during sexual relationship enhance emotional intimacy and calmness. Lovemaking that is mutually fulfilling emotionally can increase the level of commitment to the relationship and couples are more likely to stay together.

Sex in marriage is great, but only if it provides mutual satisfaction to both partners and each other's sexual desires are fulfilled. Unfortunately husbands and wives tend to react differently to sex: while the wife places greater emphasis on the emotional aspects of intimacy as an expression of love, the husband is more physical and regards sex as central to the marital relationship. One famous preacher defines the wife as a crock pot and the man as a microwave: she takes her time while he is in a hurry. This often leads to increasing passivity and ultimate boredom on the part of the wife, and the husband needs to be considerate in ensuring that the enjoyment is mutual. Also, the husband is often depicted as sexually insatiable but this is in fact not true: most women also have strong sexual drive, though subdued over time by societal norm that sex is the husband's initiative. A good husband should encourage his wife to seize the initiative as desired, and either partner should respond positively to the other even when he/she is not in the mood. The bible says that spouses should put the needs and interests of their partners ahead of theirs: "*The wife's body does not belong to her alone but also to her husband.*

In the same way, the husband's body does not belong to him alone but also to his wife. Do not deprive each other except by mutual consent and for a time, so that you may devote yourselves to prayer". 1 Corinthians 7:3-5.

Sex can quickly become relegated in marriage for many reasons: arrival of children, work stress, the demands of running a home, etc., and the rate of decline is usually faster for the wife who bears the heavy load of raising children. Husbands often complain that their wives simply shift their emotions to the first new addition to the family and they become increasingly unimportant as more children arrive. Statistics show that couples have sex around two to three times a week in the first few years of marriage, around three times a month by the first decade, and a few times a year for those who have been married over forty years. This decline does not necessarily indicate a deteriorating marital relationship, in fact, it may mean that couples have developed many other intimate ways of connecting emotionally over time, they have succeeded in growing a loving, stable, mature relationship which keeps growing strong with or without sex. It should be noted also that there could be physical, medical or psychological conditions that can limit the sexual desire or ability of either partner. Couples who are physically capable should strive to maintain a healthy, mutually satisfying sex life as long as they live. However, partners who failed to develop intimate and emotional connection in the early years of marriage will live like strangers in later life (if they remain together). A wife whose emotional and sexual needs are not adequately fulfilled may become passive or even look out of the marriage, while passivity of the wife especially early in the marriage is a prominent excuse for the husband's infidelity. It is vital also that partners make concerted effort to remain physically attractive to each other.

4.16 MANAGING MIDLIFE CRISIS

At some point in the life of many individuals, the status quo of family life no longer brings satisfaction and a psychological crisis sets in, known as *midlife crisis* because it occurs most frequently in middle-aged individuals, typically 45-64 years old (Wikipedia 2019, Chernoff 2015, Chandra 2011). A transition of identity or self-confidence may occur, triggered by many stressors including obvious physical effects of ageing, stagnation, shortcomings of achievement in life, boredom, inevitable mortality, and this could lead to feelings of depression, remorse, anxiety, irritability, and general dissatisfaction with life. Effects include the desire to make drastic changes to a person's current lifestyle, including attempts to reverse the physical effects of ageing, flirting or even walking away from an apparently happy, stable marriage.

Problems also arise from career setback, or loss of a loved one, although this can also happen earlier or later in life. It is important to note the difference between this problem and mid-life *stressor* which most couples experience due to a diverse range of day-to-day stressors over many years due to the multi-dimensional roles as wives or husbands, mothers or fathers, employees or employers, extended family issues, all which add up, causing what psychologists often refer to as "overload". In any case, mid-life is always a time for reflection and self-reassessment but is not always accompanied by the psychological upheaval associated with mid-life crisis. Research indicates that mid-life crisis may be mainly a cultural construct since it has been found to be less common in the more traditional societies. Also, while both men and women are susceptible, the triggers as well as the reactions are different.

Ageing (and associated physical changes) is a prime cause of midlife-crisis, often aggravated by issues with work/career, spousal relationships, unconsummated marriage, maturation and exit of children from homes, aging or death of parents, etc. Men often express their frustration through irrational decisions, including unjustifiable expenses or seeking relationships with younger women. Women tend to evaluate their achievement vis-à-vis their input and sacrifices, often leading to an intense feeling of under-achievement, failure or disappointment. This may lead to depression or a decision to leave a 2-3 decade old marriage, not necessarily due to a new relationship. In many relationships, the husband remains peripheral to the mainstream family life for many years, largely pursuing his own interests, or as a result of employment demand. The negative effect on his wife is mitigated by the presence of children who keep her very busy. However, once they leave home (the woman is in her mid-forties), she has plenty of time for self-reassessment and loneliness sets in, often leading to depression.

Some of the causes of midlife crisis are not under the control of either partner in a marital relationship: like ageing, job loss, illness, childlessness, loss of loved ones, etc. However, there is a lot that can be done to minimize potential causes or mitigate the potentially devastating effects. For example, women should realize that the dynamics of interest in marital relationships are in opposite directions compared with their husbands': for women, growth in interest is slow but steady (crock pot), for men it is microwave-speed – instant, intense, but short-lived, often at peak in the first few sexual encounters. In effect, many husbands stay committed to relationships and marital vows not because of sex but due to the totality of the home environment: growing intimacy with their wives; homely environment; arrival of loving children; support from their partners in stressful situations; and and wives can do a lot to make this happen. On the other hand, husbands need to be less selfish in promoting solely their interest and should do more to nurture mutual interests; they need to stop seeing their wives purely as sex objects, home carers and child minders, but as valuable life partners and best friends. Only then can a couple expect their relationship to become mature, resilient and midlife syndrome-resistant.

5   Raising children and parenting

5.1   INTRODUCTION

Children are gifts from God, and a couple must learn to accept situations as God's will. Arrival of children brings great joy to the family (and new challenges), and, for most families, the team is complete by the end of the first ten years. However, growing the family comes with formidable challenges which couples deal with for the next two decades, from sleepless nights to dealing with frequent illnesses and health challenges, financial stresses, education, parenting and different phases of behavioral issues. For many, there is joy at the end of it all, but the traditional concept of relying on children for support in old age (which makes people prefer male children) is becoming increasingly obsolete. The modern world also has major challenges and relatively few earn enough to meet their immediate family needs. Every couple wants to have children, although in some modern cultures, couples decide otherwise. In fact, in many cultures, non-consummation of a marriage, secondary infertility, or failure to have a male child is often the startup of a failed marriage, and the wife carries sole responsibility because it is inconceivable that the man could be the problem. Pressure starts to mount on the husband mostly from his family to seek a more productive wife. This is a major test of a couple's solidarity and unity in resisting all pressures from all sources.

5.2   RAISING CHILDREN

Every child is a valuable gift from God, fully endowed with virtues (and quite a few issues as well), and there as many different DNAs as there are children. One of the qualities of good parents is the ability to spot and sharpen the virtues of each child, while working as humanely as possible with the child to overcome the issues. One of the monumental mistakes that parents make is to anoint any child as a favorite: every child should be a favorite. This does not mean that one or two children (especially the middle ones) will not feel marginalized, and parents need to develop empathy and reassurance strategies. It is vital that couples realize from the beginning that children are not the primary prize of commitment to each other. If it were, a childless marriage is doomed. The arrival of children is a God-given gift meant to complement and consolidate a deep mutual relationship between man and woman. Children are to be loved and cared for, but they do not take precedence over commitment to each other. Parents often make a tragic mistake of committing their total devotion to their children at the expense of their spouses. Remember that the children are going to leave home sooner or later (and some don't even look back) and who will be left? You and your spouse.

The era of wanting as many children as possible is over: it was regarded as an insurance against old age since at least some would be around to look after their parents. In earlier times, men needed as many hands as possible on their farms, so they married many wives and had many children. Furthermore child mortality was high and having as many as possible ensured that at least some would survive. Clearly, this is no longer tenable since child mortality has dropped significantly. Also, children can (and often do) decide to relocate to very distant places, and are hardly ever in a position to carry parents' social and financial burden. It is vital that a couple plans the size of family they desire from the start. Every addition to the family brings abundant joy and abundant stress on a couple's time, careers, finances, and even relationship. While some parents may be able to afford hiring help, a nanny is never a good substitute for a mother for many reasons. Furthermore, raising children has become a very expensive process and a potentially major stressor in managing a family's finances. Bringing to the world a child that cannot be properly cared for is irresponsible and the consequences on both the couple and the child can be devastating. Parents who bring to life more children than they can properly care for often spend the last phase of their lives in penury because they never had a chance to prepare for the future, yet there is no guarantee that any of the children will be there for them. In the words of Michael Youssef (2016), " to pass on spiritual and moral values requires time, lifestyle modeling and unconditional love with no favoritism", and parents need to make time for adequate parenting of their children in spite of the increasing challenges. Furthermore, parents need to be in good standing with their faith, only then can they be capable of meeting their children's spiritual needs. Children are very brilliant copycats (of both the good and the bad), if parents lead the walk of faith, they will follow.

Ample research evidence on human development shows clearly that children develop from early in life a lot of instincts that will largely dominate their later life - like concern for others, empathy, compassion, values, faith, rudeness, aggression, etc. They are adults-in-the-making and parents need to work hard and consistently to guide and nurture the positive instincts and help overcome the negative ones in order to help them become happy, responsible and successful adults, and virtuous citizens. They should be adequately equipped to cope with and manage social and workplace relationships which are a key ingredient of a happy life. They should be well-prepared to resist the disruptive, caustic peer and role models that they will inevitably interact with once they start school and interacting with others.

5.3   PARENTING

Parenting is the process of helping your children develop physically, emotionally and intellectually from infancy to adulthood. It is the process of inculcating in the child the right values, like good behavior, learning to live in peace with siblings, respect for others, and learning to manage money from an early age. What parents consider the right values vary widely between cultures and social stratifications but the primary goal of parenting practices all over the world is to do all that is possible to ensure that children grow in a healthy, stable, loving environment, and are well prepared for life as productive and responsible adults. Children need inspiration, encouragement and support to master key developmental tasks. For a three-child family, this means the devotion of around twenty five years of a couple's prime time before the last child leaves home for college.

One of the greatest frustrations for parents and sources of disappointments in later life is to see their children as failed products in spite of their efforts. However, while children can still become failed adults in spite of the best parenting, much of the problems that surface in later life were in fact seeded from the early years through faulty parenting. For example, families are beginning to outsource parenting responsibilities to daycare, nurseries and schools, whereas a parent is the child's first contact with the world and the best role model. Working parents are finding it increasingly difficult to devote enough time to parenting and send their children to daycare from as early as six months. Exposure of the child to external influence from a very early age can in fact cause parenting problems - mixing with children who bring different values from different homes and backgrounds, etc. The proper role of the parent is to provide encouragement, support, and access to activities that enable the child master key developmental tasks. Parents are their children's first and best teachers and should remain their best teacher throughout life.

5.3.1   Parenting skills

Acquiring the right skills is a steep learning curve with changing variables. In fact, it is one of the best management training programs around. However, development of children is in phases and by the time you have achieved a decent level of competence in managing one phase, they have moved on; and when you feel that you now know all there is about parenting, you find that you don't need the skills anymore because they have all left home! Many parents lack parenting skills and believe it starts and ends with providing for the child's care and needs while others try to apply 'old style' skills to modern parenting.

5.3.2   Killing your child softly with love

All children are born flawed and delinquent (inherited from their parents !), with the propensity to sin and rebel and, no matter how much you love your child, firm, fair and corrective discipline should be part of the core values for effective parenting. All parents develop intense love for their off-springs; they want the best for them; they want their children to succeed in life. However, parent-child love is like a double-edged sword: it can be profoundly helpful in the holistic development of the child, or it can be harmful. Love that is infused with strict values and discipline is very beneficial to the child. However, it is easy to unintentionally and inadvertently destroy a child on account of uncontrolled and misdirected love, which may manifest as overprotection, permissiveness, a blurred vision between right and wrong, and excessive freedom, all of which are characteristic of a spoilt child and have potentially damaging effect on the preparedness of the child for adulthood. It is not difficult to see why many people who have been outstandingly successful in their own careers end up raising failed children: apart from the tendency to be over-permissive and spoil their children, they are often so intensely involved in pursuing their own career goals that the child gets little or no parental tutoring. The old saying, "spare the rod, spoil the child" is relevant here especially when modernized: "love your children, spank them". Spanking in the modern context does not necessarily mean flogging: there are many more effective ways of correcting a child, promoting the ability to distinguish between right and wrong values, and inculcating discipline.

5.3.3   Parenting style

The number of stressors in parenting has multiplied exponentially: work/life balance, finance, health issues, external influences especially the social media, and many more but parents' stress tolerance and response capabilities have not been able to keep pace. Nevertheless and in spite of the formidable challenges, parenting is very satisfying and fulfilling if you succeed in raising children of good character and strong faith, well prepared and equipped to face the numerous trials and challenges of modern life. Parenting is a two-way process where you learn from each other: as your children learn from you, so they inspire you to sharpen your creativity, patience and tolerance levels; you learn to give up many of your own needs and desires in favor of their needs; you learn the art of corrective discipline. One of the many problems of parenting is that each child keeps changing, and by the time you think you mastered dealing with one stage, they have moved to another.

Parenting is particularly hard for modern couples who were raised in strict traditional homes but now have to raise their own children in an environment that is too infectious, permissive and indulgent. One exasperated parent recently declared: "I think parenting is very different now. We're totally governed by our children." Nevertheless, by deciding to have a child, parents have implicitly committed themselves to creating an environment in which the child can develop strong values and good character, and work starts from the time the child is a baby; they now need to develop modern skills of parenting. In fact many parents attend extramural classes and read widely on parenting. In the words of Milton Sapirstein (1963), "education, like neurosis begins at home." Parents who seed the early character building of their children to the child minder or school will have a lot to regret in future. They need to remember that, in spite of difficulties and complexities, it is a lot easier to raise children with strong character than to repair broken adults who bring nothing but misery to negligent parents in later life. While appropriate parenting is crucial in helping a child to develop life skills, there are other influences and factors that determine the future character of the child other than parenting, for example, the child's DNA and temperament, and peer group influence. Every child has a different character, different assets, and different challenges even when they are siblings, and one cap does not fit all in dealing with them. It is astounding the number of parents who don't even know the assets, strong points and weaknesses of their offspring, hence they are of little help in getting the child to develop in a holistic manner and stimulating the child to develop career goals.

Parents need to evaluate their children and devise strategies for helping each child to develop good interpersonal relationships from a young age, overcome any deficiencies, and evolve personal life achievement goals. Some parents make the mistake of choosing careers for their children; this can be counter-productive especially when they have no aptitude. Subtle ways are far more effective: if for example you would like your child to become a doctor or an engineer, do a lot to help strengthen his/her interest and competence in STEM (science, technology, engineering, math) subjects by complementing regular school education.

Parenting styles vary a lot between families and across cultures. Parents have different levels of expectations, set standards of behavior and performance demands from their children, and different styles of encouragement and discipline to ensure compliance. Parents need strong relationship skills and competence in stress management in order to manage the complexity of evolving a right balance between showing love, helping the child to develop the right behavioral skills and independent thinking, and enforcing discipline. However, in spite of the diversity in parenting styles, there are some commonalities which have been used to classify parenting styles into four categories known as Baumrind parenting styles:

- **Authoritarian or Disciplinarian:** set behavioral rules are strictly enforced, with disciplinary consequences for deviation. There is little or no room for negotiation.

- **Permissive Parenting:** parents mostly let children have their way, with limited intervention in terms of guidance, rules, or discipline for misbehavior.

- **Uninvolved Parenting**: children have freedom to decide on what they do, when and how they do it, with little or no interference from parents. This often happens out of ignorance or the fact that parents are too busy dealing with more urgent issues of their own.

- **Authoritative Parenting:** parents are caring and nurturing but deal firmly with misbehavior. They love their children passionately but not at the expense of discipline. Rather than spoon-feed children, they help them develop initiatives, independent thinking, self-discipline and personal goals, with subtle but effective parental communication, guidance and rewards. This style is believed to be the most effective and beneficial to children.

5.3.4   Child discipline

Discipline is often regarded as synonymous with punishment. This is in fact not true. Discipline is about helping a child learn how to behave appropriately and how not to behave, and there are many age-appropriate disciplinary strategies that do not include punishment and yet are very effective. Children need to know what behavior is acceptable, whether at home, at school or anywhere else; they need to learn to develop appropriate relationship skills, like the ability to get along with others; they also need to learn how to manage provocative situations, such as sibling disagreement or bullying. Too little discipline as a child could lead to negative behavioral issues as adults, while too harsh or negative discipline often damages children's self-esteem and confidence in later life, and can promote aggressive behavior. Discipline works best when it is corrective, firm and fair, when parents go to great length to make the child appreciate set limits, why the limits are necessary, and consequences for violation.

Discipline should start with babies, even though they don't really understand right from wrong. Babies learn quite quickly the power of crying and often use it effectively to get their way. They know that crying will set several people running to attend to them and, if not well managed, there will be delays in settling to routines which can be very stressful. For example, a baby who gets used to being held before it can fall asleep will deprive parents of much-needed night rest. Subtle discipline involves helping babies to settle to routines in terms of feeding and sleeping, once everything has been done to make them comfortable. Between the ages of one to three, toddlers start to learn more about cause and effects, and the effectiveness of throwing tantrums to get their way. Parents need to develop disciplinary strategies, like depriving them temporarily of something they like, such as a favorite toy, enforcing a short time-out, or having a conversation. Parents who practice this model will be surprised how quickly the child pipes down when threatened with any of these simple disciplinary measures.

Preschoolers in the 3-5 age group are perhaps the most difficult group to deal with. They have a good understanding of what behavior is acceptable and what is not; they become exposed to children from different backgrounds in play groups or pre-schools and learn a lot from them. By the time they reach school age, they know what behavior they can get away with at home but not at school; they use tantrums to try and get their way; and parents often find them the most difficult to manage. In some schools children in the first grade are taught how to call the police if they feel they are being abused. While this is designed to protect them from child abuse, the child can quickly interpret abuse to include simple discipline as insisting on 'no TV before homework.' Parents need to establish authority from an early age and leave the child in no doubt who is in charge. Time-outs, which should be developmentally appropriate, supervised and brief, lasting for only a few minutes has been found to be very effective in moderating their misbehavior. Also, once they see that parents stand their ground, they quickly back off.

Managing adolescent children is perhaps the bumpiest of parental ride. It is as if rebellion is a prominent part of their school curriculum. It is an age in which children begin to assert themselves, their independence, their privacy, and the difference between right and wrong becomes blurred. Parents need a mature and patient approach and excellent communication skills to reach a typical adolescent. Perhaps the greatest satisfaction of parents in later life is an opportunity to watch their children raise their own adolescents, dealing with the same issues as parents had with them.

Child discipline and acceptable practices are greatly influenced by personal, cultural, religious and societal values. Historically, the use of corporal punishment was widely accepted, and still is in some conservative societies although the practice has been dropped or outlawed in some developed societies. According to psychologists, physical punishment might get children to behave well out of fear but it is an ineffective way of correcting a child and can often lead to problems with self-esteem and anxiety in later life. Furthermore, it could lead a child to believe that physical abuse is legitimate and could enhance aggressive behavior in later life. While most parents no longer spank their children, many find that the threat of a spank is enough to stop a child from misbehaving.

5.3.5   Shared parenting

Parenting is most effective when both parents are involved and agreeable. If two very different people pool their DNA, they'll create more genetic variety that creates a much richer, conducive home atmosphere for raising children. The traditional role of the husband as the bread winner with limited contributions to social reproduction implies that the wife has to bear the burden of child raising, and this model is no longer tenable in the modern context, in view of the fact that many women are also working. Furthermore, the active presence of a Dad in a home has a significant psychological impact on children, in particular, male children. Both parents need to be closely involved in order to provide a well-balanced experience for the children. Joint parenting is very effective for instilling a foundation of values on which the future lives of the children will be built. The most overwhelming key to a child's success is the positive involvement of both parents in the process of upbringing. Statistics show that children that are raised in a home with a married mother and father both intimately involved in their upbringing consistently do better in every measure of well-being than their peers who come from divorced, step-parent, single-parent, blended, or cohabiting homes. Dads can become self-absorbed, pursuing their own interests intensely: career, golf, club activities, etc., to the extent that they become absentee daddies and fail to make the right impact on the life of the growing child. In fact, just like in families in which most parents grew up, many children still have too much of mothers and too little of daddies in many families across all cultures.

Children are astute politicians, and they display it from day one: the newborn baby quickly learns the power of crying as a very effective way of getting his/her way; children will try all tactics, including playing parents against each other to get their way. It is vital therefore that parents remain on the same page on important decisions concerning their children. It is important also to note that children go through different phases of development, from tantrum to rebellion, and parents also need to change tactics. The modern environment is becoming increasingly toxic and hostile to effective parenting, with children being exposed at very early ages to drugs, pornography, peer influence, and the ubiquitous 'social media syndrome'. Statistics show that teenagers spend about nine hours a day on the screen (cell phone, minipads, laptops, television, etc. and this is beginning to affect their self-esteem and mental stability, often causing depression which has led to suicide in some cases. There have been several deaths of teenagers by suicide as a result of cyberbullying or visits to toxic sites such as those that share content on depression, anxiety, self-harm, suicide, inappropriate sex, etc. Also, social media bullying is on the rise and has been linked to the rising rate of suicide among young children. Several recent studies have shown a significant increase in cyberbullying of on-line 5-to-15 year-olds in recent years, and the negative effects on their mental health have increased markedly. Several countries are already planning actions including imposing new rules on social media and introducing mindfulness exercises in schools. Parents have a monumental task of controlling and moderating their children's exposure to these damaging 'infections.' However, many parents are also infected and addicted, spending similar periods watching the TV, playing virtual games, on cell phones, or twitting, and discipline needs to start with them.

The Christian faith and indeed most other faiths have strong moral doctrines which a child needs to be exposed to without coercion from an early age. There is a very wide range of free age-appropriate Christian literature and on-line content on parenting and child psychology to select from; access to children's Sunday school helps a lot; and family prayers that give five-year olds opportunities to pray and express their thankfulness and wishes directly to God can help develop a child's desire to know more about Christian faith in later life. Some families hold Saturday-evening family bible classes in which each child takes turn to lead discussions on their favorite bible passages, and all family members pray in turn. Again, adolescence is the most challenging time to nurture a child's faith. This is the phase in which they start to question the essence of faith in the light of happenings around them. Quite often it is a passing phase but could result in irreversible damage unless parents develop strategies and devote time to help them through this trying period.

5.3.6   Do as I do, not as I say

Parents are first-level role models for their children. the way they dress, walk, talk, eat, treat each other, and they need to 'rule by example', conscious of the fact that children will probably copy 'the good, the bad, and the ugly.'. it is inevitable (it is even healthy) that parents will have hot arguments irrespective of the longevity of their marriage, but, 'never in front of the children.' In the words of a writer (Charles Swindoll): "each day of our lives we make deposits in the memory banks of our children." Another writer (Robert Fulgum) cautions: "don't worry that children never listen to you; worry that they are always watching you,"

By and large, husbands are beginning to re-tune to the new realities of sharing household responsibilities with their wives, and helping to involve their children. This development also creates an indelible impression on their young children. It is vital that children are well prepared for the modern world from an early age by introducing them to all aspects of modern living, starting with keeping their rooms tidy, and getting involved in household chores from cooking to doing the laundry. In many traditional cultures, getting a male child to do any household chore is a taboo, but this becomes a major problem in future when he lives with a working wife. The millennial child (male or female) knows very little about running a home (the house-help or mother does it all), and this becomes a major issue in later life for most couples who cannot afford domestic help or total dependence on 'eating out' which is unhealthy anyway. Most modern couples now share household chores: when the wife is cooking, the husband is busy with laundry or vacuuming the carpet (thanks to modern appliances), helping with children's homework, preparing them for bed or school, or taking them to school or recreation events. Many modern husbands are also excellent cooks.

5.3.7   Managing work-parenting challenges

The tradition in which the husband is the provider and the wife the home-maker is fast disappearing with the empowerment of women. Many women are now well educated, economically empowered and career oriented. While most families benefit significantly from the added earning power of the matriarch, managing work-life issues with parenting can pose formidable challenges to family stability to the extent of causing the break up of the marriage. Many women would rather stay home and look after their children, in fact, a recent study showed that half of the 80 million American mums are stay-home mums. However, many are haunted by potential challenges posed by the unexpected: like the husband losing his job, becoming incapacitated, dying or walking away from the marriage. While managing work-life career is often a prominent topic during courtship, the full implications are rarely obvious until reality sets in.

Couples need to discuss possible ways of managing work-life issues preferably during courtship, but certainly at the beginning of a marriage. The best-paying jobs may not be in the best interest of the family and couples, especially wives should be prepared to make sacrifices in choosing jobs that allow for some degree of flexibility, like working partly or fully from home, or self-employment, even if it means learning new skills or stepping down in remuneration. However, when the wife also has high earning power, it means that the family can afford options that provide some flexibility for the family, like paying for the school bus, after-school activities or the occasional child minder. However, they still need to ensure that enough time is devoted to parenting.

Many women choose to take time off their careers to raise children, but this also poses new challenges: the world is on fast track and just three years away from a career may make re-integration very difficult. Fortunately, some employers now provide retraining programs to help women get back on their career lines after time-off, and many are providing work-place creches to ease their parenting problems. The common practice for a career couple is that the husband seeks the best job available, and the wife tries to fit in by looking for employment in the same area. It is more productive if family interest features prominently among variables for consideration in accepting job offers: for example, proximity to family-friendly areas of abode in terms of good schools and good neighbor-hoods.

Core Values in Parenting

"Parenting is one of the hardest jobs on earth". —*Jennifer Aniston*

"Parenting is one of the best management training programs there is".—*Irene Rosenfeld*

"There is no such thing as a perfect parent. So just be a real one." — *Sue Atkins*

"Parenting is not giving your child everything they want. Parenting is not being your child's friend. Parenting is about preparing your child to be a useful and respectful person in society". — *GloZell*

"Where parents do too much for their children, the children will not do much for themselves."
—*Elbert Hubbard*

"At the end of the day, the most overwhelming key to a child's success is the positive involvement of parents". — *Jane D. Hull*

"The kids who need the most love will ask for it in the most unloving ways."
— *Russel Barkley*

"Whatever you would have your children become, strive to exhibit in your own lives and conversation." — *Lydia H. Sigourney*

"Children are not casual guests in our home. They have been loaned to us temporarily for the purpose of loving them and instilling a foundation of values on which their future lives will be built".— *James Dobson*

"You can learn many things from children. How much patience you have, for instance".
— *Franklin P. Jones*

"The number of stressors has multiplied exponentially: traffic, money, success, work/life balance, the economy, the environment, parenting, family conflict, relationships, disease. As the nature of human life has become far more complicated, our ancient stress response hasn't been able to keep up" — *Andrew J. Bernstein*

"Parenting now is a two-way relationship where you learn from each other"
— *Juhi Chawla*

"There's really no point in having children if you're not going to be home enough to father them". — *Anthony Edwards*

"What lingers from the parent's individual past, unresolved or incomplete, often becomes part of her or his irrational parenting" — *Virginia Satir*

"Even as kids reach adolescence, they need more than ever for us to watch over them. Adolescence is not about letting go. It's about hanging on during a very bumpy ride".
— *Ron Taffel*

"Few things are more satisfying than seeing your children have teenagers of their own".
— *Doug Larson*

6 Potential pitfalls in marriage

6.1 INTRODUCTION

Marriage is designed to putatively last until death but vows are being increasingly cut short by irreconcilable differences which ultimately lead to divorce. In the words of a psychologist, "personalities change, bodies change and romantic love waxes and wanes." Conflict in marriage is normal, inevitable, even healthy: what enables a marriage to endure is how couples handle conflict situations. There is a widespread misconception that marriage is bliss, and many are caught unawares and unprepared when the numerous trials and tribulations start to appear. The bliss comes if and when a couple succeeds in surmounting these problems, very much like the calm that prevails after a turbulent phase of a ship's journey on the oceans. Marriage is like God leading you to the Jordan; through faith and perseverance, He will create a way to cross it; the promised land is on the other side.

6.2 MARRIAGE IS SMOOTH SAILING? BRACE YOURSELVES FOR HURRICANES, TORNADOES AND TSUNAMIS

It was indeed a tsunami that transformed marriage from what God meant it to be and produced the first dysfunctional family. But thanks be to God, He reinstated joy and happiness in marriage when He sent His Only Begotten Son to redeem mankind from the attack of the serpent. The attack deprived Adam and Eve of marital satisfaction, Adam's intimacy with God and his spouse Eve, disrupted their economic base and imposed wrong conceptions of womanhood/manhood. As observed by Jacquelin and Daniel Hanselman (2017), Adam refused to listen to his wife because she caused him to be estranged from God. He withheld good from her because of his grief over loosing intimacy with God. This submissive role pervaded the lives of Isaac and Rebecca and still does in many cultures of the world today, leading to a distorted image of the husband and complementarity of the couple. The New Testament with the teachings of Jesus Christ and the Apostles provided the basis for a shift to the original concept of marriage (partnership with different roles), how a tsunami can be avoided, tornadoes and hurricanes minimized. The more the satisfaction in marriage, the less the likelihood of actions that cause a break because intimacy, passion and commitment work together to make it smooth sailing. However, marital conflict is a reality with different levels of severity. It is an inevitable part of the relationship that should enhance rather than destroy it; it will remain prominent throughout marital life, although in differing shades and intensities.

There are several fundamental realities in conflict issues, notably: couples are different but complementary and should know the basic differences, accept and adjust to them; couples should learn the basic biological and gender differences, those that are fixed and those that can be changed; you should never try to change your partner to become a carbon copy of your flawed self. While it is often assumed that divorce is usually the result of severe problems between couples such as abuse, adultery, desertion, research shows that nearly 90% of conflicts that end in divorce are non-severe: financial issues, parenting, sexual relationship, etc. Disagreements are often emotional and momentary, the end is unpredictable, and the fallouts can be traumatic in a relationship. Jimmy and Karen Evans (2019) provide an extensive analysis of emotional issues and personality traits that can threaten relationships if not appreciated by the couple. For example, the focus and style of the task-oriented person differ significantly from those of the people-oriented: while one is good at getting things done the other usually adds spice and variety to the relationship. Both work for the relationship and need to be appreciated and rescued from selfish instincts that make us feel that one is better than the other. Not only do we need to see the good in each other, we must learn to give up, give in and give all. To resolve a conflict, it is necessary to consider and never be dismissive of your partner's standpoint to make progress. Both need to learn to lay aside hurt, anger and bitterness to bring the relationship to equilibrium daily.

Jimmy and Karen recommend several standing rules and commitments for peaceful living (see Table 6.1). Suggestions include maintaining fellowship daily, avoiding confrontation, harassment, and running your partner down. People have different ways of making a case. Couples are therefore advised to concentrate on the problem not the person, on behavior instead of character, on facts rather than judging motives.

Table 6.1 Ten marriage decisions couples should make to save their marriage. *(Jimmy Evans (2019)*

- We will never threaten divorce.
- We will never go to bed angry.
- We will never "agree to disagree."
- We will respect and celebrate our differences
- We will give each other the right to complain and be honest without paying a price.
- We will be faithful to each other.
- We will develop healthy relationships with fellow believers.
- We will make our decisions together.
- Apart from our relationship with God, we will prioritize our marriage above everything else.
- We will base our marriage on Christ-like love.

Having a listening ear and an understanding heart breaks the selfish instincts and provides the level playing field for issues to be discussed. This means couples should listen to each other's opinions so that the best decisions can be taken. Gone are the days when the man had the last word and women are treated as chattel. The issues in a conflict often resuscitate earlier unresolved disagreements, making the resolution of a conflict difficult. The advice therefore is to discuss and try to fully resolve one issue at a time. Discussions should be held at an appropriate time and place and not when there are emotional states which are disruptive of conflict resolution. Anger, irritation, fatigue, a highly emotional state, tension, being defensive, sensitive, unhappy and overwhelmed threaten conflict resolution. Couples should develop preemptive withdrawal strategies, such as cutting an escalating argument and coming back to the issue when both have had time to cool down.

Resolving conflict requires forgiveness, a difficult state spiritually and practically. Do not design punishment for every disagreement and do not show resentment, avoid making judgements suggesting that you are Mr. or Mrs Perfect. Marriage experts and those with long years of experience advice that you return a blessing for an insult although it may cause tearful eyes. Couples are advised to plan their trip to a happy marriage giving enough time to discuss conflict resolution skills to avoid the popular fight, flight and freeze behavior that leads the union aground. When supported by scriptures and constant reminder of the divine nature of marriage, resolving conflict could be done with love, mutual respect and fun. Always remember that you could be wrong and be prepared to apologize and or accept an apology.

The issues that cause conflict could be small or big issues. The advice is that you drop them in the trash once they are resolved. If they are kept in left luggage, they will always lead to something more difficult to settle. Conflict is good, it promotes connection, and there will be plenty of disagreements throughout marital life, often starting from day one and persisting to the mature healthy marriage. In fact, when a relationship is devoid of conflict it could mean that couples have given up on each other. However, how conflicts are dealt with and resolved is crucial, starting with a "no winner, no looser" concept, because you will either win together or lose together every time. Both partners should fight for connection, not knockout. Men and women talk and think differently, and relationships should not disintegrate because of the differences. Rather, couples should learn to work together to resolve differences by trying to appreciate the standpoint of one another. Couples should not try to avoid a potentially disruptive problem by sweeping it under the carpet, or practice appeasement. Neither ever works; the problem will resurface, often on a higher tempo. Also, aggression is forbidden in a marital relationship, couples need to develop a strategy for attacking problems and issues, not one another.

Negativity is undesirable in marriage: 'you'll never change… this marriage can never work…" If one partner has concluded that things and situations can never change, there is no real reason or need for the other to try. Acceptance, accommodation and adjustment are very effective instruments for strengthening marriages. Some habits simply will not change, and every spouse has to learn to accept that in their partners. In effect, each partner needs to develop coping mechanisms. Quite often, patience and accommodation can work wonders. Let both start with you and watch the positive effect on your partner. By accommodating, you change; by accepting, you resign yourself to the situation; by adjusting, both of you change.

Couples need to set "red lines" which they will always endeavor not to cross, like quarreling in front of the children, resorting to use of caustic words or physical combat, or engaging in endless arguments. Words exchanged during conflicts can have far-reaching and lingering consequences. Words, like a broken egg cannot be retracted and you never need to defend what you did not say; words can be misinterpreted or twisted and every bad word from one incites a worse response from the other. In the words of Yejuda Berg, "Words are singularly the most powerful force available to humanity. We can choose to use this force constructively with words of encouragement, or destructively using words of despair. Words have energy and power with the ability to help, to heal, to hinder, to hurt, to harm, to humiliate and to humble". Most often, words convey your thoughts and emotions but, it is not uncommon for a couple to say things they don't really mean during arguments, just to score a point. It is quite common to say words like " I knew marrying you was a mistake... you are simply no good...this marriage will never work". However, in the words of Joyce Meyer (2015), "words are containers of power. This marriage is simply not going to work.....I absolutely cannot put up with this anymore......If one more thing happens, I'm leaving". By saying hurtful words even if you don't mean them, you have already delivered the energy and the damage is done. Couples should read Joyce Meyer's book on the power of words, there is a lot they can learn about managing conflicts. One partner needs to call a stop, and the woman is more gifted, (or less conceited). Humility is a gift but can also be acquired, and both partners need it to concretize their relationship. One couple who had been happily married for five decades Christened their bed 'the Center for Truth and Reconciliation', and vowed never to sleep without resolving the issues and conflicts of the day.

Every marriage is full of challenges which change in form and intensity as the marriage progresses, and remain prominent 'till death do us part.' These include resolving differences, financial issues, career issues, dealing with arrival and parenting of children, looking after parents and other relations, health issues, in-law issues and other external interferences, etc. Prepare for persecution: no matter how good you are as individuals or couples, somebody is not going to like you. In fact, those who hate you without cause or due to envy will be too many to count. Committed and devoted partnership sharpens the ability of couples to deal jointly and effectively with these issues. It needs absolute commitment to each other, exceptional wisdom, and God's grace. As relationship matures, 'my/your problem' will become 'our problem'.

6.3   LIVING APART: LEAD US NOT INTO TEMPTATION

Separation at any point in marriage is undesirable although, in some cases, may be unavoidable. For example a young, newly married man may be conscripted for a national duty that takes him out of the country without any provision for his family. This explains why people in the armed forces often find it difficult to sustain a marriage. The wife may be tempted to flirt while the husband may come back changed by the trauma of conflict. Couples also chose to accept jobs in different locations and maintain relationship by commuting (commuter marriage). Couples who choose this model are only loosely committed to the relationship and have inadvertently initiated a potential marriage breaker. While the wife may find some comfort in having the children around her, a lonely man is a vulnerable man. In situations where couples have a choice, staying together (live-together model) is by far the best option, even if it means letting better offers and opportunities pass. Even though this is not an insurance against flirting or a guarantee of an enduring marriage, it helps a lot to eliminate those temptations and vulnerabilities that are often triggered by loneliness. A third model is emerging which Sociologists call "living apart together (LAT)" in which couples simply choose not to live together, often living in different apartments within walking distance. One partner in this type of relationship recently gave a justification for this model: This arrangement, she explained, gives her space to pursue her work and hobbies, and helps them better understand what's actually going on with each other. "We enjoy this idea that there is a space we each have to ourselves that nobody else is going to enter for a period of time…… I do think it really forces communication," A partner in this type of relationship, Judith Newman, who has lived apart from her husband in the same city for around twenty five years summarized her experience in a recent book: *To Siri With Love (2017).* According to her narrative, they discovered early that his fastidiousness and her desire for children (he wasn't initially so sure) made living apart a clear choice. Keeping two separate places, even with kids, would actually give them more space and could even be cheaper. Plus, she adds, it's made their relationship possible. "[Some] people get married or start to live with each other, and all of these qualities they find wonderful rub up against the ones that aren't supportable on a day-to-day basis," she says. "If they didn't have to do that, they'd probably be very happy together." Some psychologists have supported LAT as a way to play to the strengths of the relationship without succumbing to its weaknesses (see Finkel 2017)". This LAT model is becoming increasingly common among younger couples for reasons that range from wanting more autonomy to just liking their own place and choosing to keep it.

6.4   MANAGING EXTERNAL INTERFERENCE

Man is a social animal and needs other human beings to survive starting with the spouse and followed by children. Because of the emphasis on the survival of this unit, God mandated it should be separated from the families of origin. Often without realizing it, external influences can have a profound impact on our lives: everything we do, our judgements, our decisions, our desire be like the Jones', etc. The influence may vary from the inspiration to conform and imitate others around us, or, perhaps less often, to avoid particular choices and behaviors of others which we consider inappropriate. Apart from this subtle type of influence which psychologists call "invisible influence" (see Berger 2016), people around you can seek to force their opinions, views and values on you: extended family members feel that have a say on how you run your marriage and home; friends feel they have a solution to your problems and issues; marriage counselors promote traditional marriage models which are no longer relevant in the context of modern relationships. Unfortunately, many of these influences are toxic in a marriage. There are other potential sources of interference: interaction with friends and acquaintances, workplace colleagues, social media, even members of groups that you fellowship with. Considering the many gory stories of intrusive external interferences in marriage, the separation of your nuclear family from all possible potential external interferences is the beginning of wisdom.

The fundamental weapon against intrusive meddling is that couples reserve the most critical issues for each other and avoid discussing their differences with others, including social media. The truth is that no other person has the listening ear and the heart to understand what the issues are. Issues are magnified, underestimated, distorted inadvertently or deliberately. It is unrealistic to expect people to love you because you are successful: your blessings are increasingly bountiful, so are your adversaries and detractors. Another basic rule which is difficult to operationalize is not to discuss your spouse, with the extended family or indeed anyone else including your close friends. Good news about your spouse will generate envy while bad news will open up an avenue for external interference in your relationship. It is possible to develop your relationship to such a level that you can internalize the resolution of disagreements, and there are testimonies from couples who have been married for five to six decades and have never had to depend on any external sources to resolve their disputes. In the event of intractable problems which defy internal resolution, couples need to exercise great discretion on where to seek help. Relations, friends and inexperienced counselors often make matters worse. Above all, both of you must learn to stand your ground together against any external interference from any source in your marriage.

6.5 DEALING WITH IN-LAWS

It is a common joke that Adam and Eve were the luckiest couple on earth, why? Because neither of them had in-laws. This is unkind to many in-laws who are very supportive of each other in an unobtrusive manner. The dynamics of in-law relationships vary greatly between families. While some accept spouses with open arms and respect, others see them as poachers who have come to reap where they did not sow, and steal their beloved son or daughter. However, in general, getting along with your in-laws is one of the greatest challenges in married life and one of the toughest relationships to navigate. Research shows that around 60% of all marriages suffer from tension with mothers-in-law, in particular, between the wife and the mother of her husband. The stereotype of the obtrusive mother-in-law has more or less become a normal part of marital life. Any in-law from either side can be obnoxious and intrusive but the husband's mother is the most stigmatized because she sees her son's house as an extension of theirs and believes her 'baby' son needs protection from an intruder; she hardly considers any woman good enough for her 'child'; she seeks to dominate the life of her son and his home, more or less dictating how things ought to be done, to the consternation of the young wife who does not have the confidence to confront her. It is not uncommon for the mother-in-law to want to dominate the marriage ceremony; she often wants to determine the choice and arrangement of furniture in her son's home, or how the young wife should run her home, her daughter-in-law's style of dressing or parenting, etc. One mother-in-law insisted that her son kept all his stuff in his family home although he could spend the night at his wife's (see Venugopal 2014). However, as the wife matures and gains confidence, confrontation becomes frequent and could lead to serious problems in the relationship. One woman sums up her frustration as follows: "I feel like an outsider when I'm around my mother-in-law. Even though my husband and I have been married 15 years, she still treats me as though I'm a threat, someone who wants to take her son away from her" (Sweat 2019), and this aptly represents the way many wives feel about their mothers-in-law. The mother and daughter-in-law relationship has tension built into it from the start: it is a bond that brings together women with different values and upbringings; they have different views on what it means to run a home and be a wife and mother. While the negative focus is on the mother-in-law, the daughter-in-law can also contribute significantly to strained in-law relationships. Many come into the relationship with the pre-conceived idea that it can never be cordial; they see as criticism and reject off hand innocent advice from the mothers-in-law; they show hostility and put a barrier in place from the start.

The daughter-mother-in-law relationship has been the subject of intense research: one psychotherapist summarizes the issue as follows: "Both parties come into it not really knowing each other and yet feel they need to form a relationship immediately. They try but usually it feels forced or it's based on very differing perspectives, which immediately puts them at odds with one another......The relationship between two women is, on average, more intimate and emotional than men's. They focus on whether they feel connected to their in-law. There is also a competitive aspect that comes into play.....Yet while you might assume this contest is for the husband or son's love, that's not the case, the competition is for the *influence* these two women have over him... It's important to remember that when your son marries, he's not bringing home a daughter. He's bringing home an adult woman; someone with her own history, her own life experiences, and her own understanding of how she wants 'family' to be. It's not that her way is right – it's that her way is different (Brann 2016)."

Unfortunately, this mother-in-law stereotype is by no means universal: many modern parents do not interfere in the marital lives of their sons and daughters and are very supportive in many ways, from babysitting to doing the school runs. Evidence abounds also that cordial relationship between women-in-law is possible. Mother-in-law and daughter-in-law can become friends, even close friends, although this connectedness can take years to develop, usually when they know a lot more about each other and initial suspicions have disappeared. There are many resource materials and Biblical stories which can help both sides in reaching this goal (Chapman 2004; Graham 2010; DeAmond 2015). Love is stronger than differences, as exemplified by the Biblical story of Ruth and Naomi, the legendary depth of connection between the two in-laws, and Ruth's declaration of commitment to her mother-in-law.

When couples take their marital vows, they are not just gaining a spouse; they are inheriting an entire family as well, and they need wisdom and God's guidance to establish healthy in-law relationships. While stories abound about overbearing in-laws, some are very valuable assets that should be nurtured, considering the support they give to busy working couples in child minding all over the world. Perhaps more than half of people who do the unpaid job of baby-sitting and school runs in the United States are grandparents who are in-laws to either spouse. This is just one of the many positive functions of in-laws. Quite often, parents-in-law end up as custodians and caregivers of children of dysfunctional marriages or where the mother is considered incapable of caring for children. Unfortunately the "mother-in-law syndrome has become so toxic that many young wives go into marital relationships, fully prepared for war with her in-laws, prompting failed in-law relationships from the start.

The family of the wife looks forward to the day their daughter will get married in spite of the fact that she will drop their family name, in fact, they worry when this is delayed. However, she is more likely than not to face hostility or rejection from her partner's family. The Biblical injunction that man shall leave his family and unite with an unknown wife is difficult for the man's family (especially his mother and sisters) to accept in societies with low status for women and the paternal home is the center of power. The Biblical injunction is also in conflict with the traditional concept that a wife is a mere addition to the husband's family. It is a common belief particularly in developing countries that a well educated wife is unlikely to be submissive or play the traditional roles of wife in the extended family hence, the economically empowered woman is rejected even where her husband is satisfied with his choice of life partner. A major problem that husbands face globally is navigating a delicate balance between protecting his wife and children from in-law hostilities and still keeping a cordial relationship with his family of origin. Unfortunately, they often end up alienating either or both. Husbands need supreme guidance, patience, perseverance and astute political skills to succeed in maintaining cordial relationships with two warring factions both of whom he loves very dearly.

In the absence of the values which encourage all participants to balance rights and responsibilities, exercise control, wives are denied the freedom given to all Christians to participate in marriage as full heirs of the kingdom. Unfortunately, marriage, the oldest institution still operates in many cultures under the traditional paradigm which projects the wife as a glorified slave in spite of the rapid socio-economic emancipation of women over the last century or so. Paternal in-laws claim their rights as occupants of a powerful estate and threaten the stability and functionality of the marriage. In some matrilineal cultures, the family of the wife can also be intrusive.

In the traditional setting, the family of a man believes that he is bringing a wife home, and it is understandable because many generations live in the same compound. Therefore, (especially for the mother-in-law), it is inconceivable and unacceptable that any woman should suddenly come between them and their son. His parents become another layer of authority to be reckoned with in the marriage. For example, in many traditional cultures, the names given to a newborn child are determined by the husband's parents. Sisters who previously shared the same home with their brothers now see the new wives as a barrier/obstruction that must be dismantled because patriarchy offers them power in the family of origin. They are a third layer of authority which interferes with the desired freedom in marriage. One would expect this to fizzle out once they too marry and face the same issues in their new homes but it usually des not.

It is very rare in any culture to see genuine cordiality between wives and their mother/sisters-in-law. Many even go to the extent of trying to replace their son's choice with their own preferences even though the new wife may eventually suffer the same fate. It is a very trying time for the husband who now has the onerous task of maintaining a happy medium, or choosing between the old and the new, and many a husband can fail woefully, either succumbing to the pressures from his family, or totally alienating them. While a man should never succumb to family pressures on his marriage, he still needs to maintain a cordial relationship with his family. One strategy that seems to work well is for the man to keep his wife and family apart as much as practicable. Some men even deliberately seek and accept jobs that take them well away from toxic extended family environment. An Italian National Statistics Institute study found that the chances of one's marriage lasting go up with every one hundred yards that a couple can put between themselves and their in-laws. Many couples have moved across country or to other countries just to save their marriage from in-laws.

Women have greater problems with in-law issues than men particularly in the traditional setting, largely because they are regarded as low-status acquisitions. They suffer from rejection, criticism and are expected to accept the traditional extended family layers of authority and control without question; they are expected to serve all members of the family and are ranked lower than the youngest child in the family, and any other wife who joined the family earlier, irrespective of age and socio-economic status; they are not entitled to family inheritance even in their own nuclear family (all properties of the nuclear family belong to their son and, by extension, to his extended family); and they cannot own property. Violence against the wife by the husband's family is common and, in the event of his demise, all his properties are transferred to his extended family. The extended family even has the traditional authority to bequeath the widowed wife to another member of the family as wife (her choice or wish is irrelevant). Even though a woman is married under modern monogamous laws, the husband's family often retains the prerogative to find a second informal wife or even expel the legal wife from their son's home if they are not pleased with her; if she fails to produce a child or a son. While some women who find themselves in this situation do not hesitate to take advantage of laws protecting their rights adding to increasing rates of divorce and separation, others find the process too frightening and simply develop coping mechanisms. Husbands also often have to deal with overbearing mother in-laws but they are usually more able to handle it in an assertive manner.

Your in-laws may not like you, and there is little you can do to impress them. However, remember that they are a crucial part of your spouse's life. This makes them a crucial part of your life as well and they deserve love and affection from you. Keep your expectations of your in-laws reasonable. Always remember that they are not your parents and that they will behave differently. It may be helpful to lower your expectations so you are less likely to become distressed. It is never easy to balance your needs with the needs of others, especially the needs of an entire new family, and there are bound to be conflicts. It helps a lot if your spouse takes the initiative to limit intrusions from his/her family since this puts you both on the same page for developing cordial relationships with your in-laws. Relations can be obtrusive, and understandably so too: they raised your partner from cradle over decades and there is a latent sense of 'ownership' and subtle domination. Couples need to deal with this problem as one and with considerable diplomacy. They should work together to put in place effective strategies for moderating in-law interference in their relationship. It should be noted however that relations are not always the cause of friction: many spouses start off with the assumption that their relationship with their in-laws will necessarily be toxic or narcissist, and are battle-ready.

Resources in MariageToday ministry recommend several ways in which the relationship with in-laws can be improved; primarily by extending the love principle that binds spouses to them, seeing them as parents, brothers and sisters who exercise the principles of rights and responsibilities. There is the need to remind in-laws to contribute to the success of the unit created by God, recognize the limits of their authority and respect the choices made by the couple. As much as possible, newly weds should not reside with extended family for extended periods of time either as hosts or guests. If this has to be in later years, in-laws should institute a cordiality code that is devoid of control and criticism. Just as a code of cordiality is important for in-law relationships, it is also necessary to regulate other relationships. Choose your friends carefully and with discretion and set decent interaction limits. Make friends with people who have your kind of values and aspirations. You cannot fly with eagles when you hang out with turkeys. Toxic friends (friendly enemies) can have a profoundly damaging influence on either partner, especially if either of you makes the monumental mistake of confiding in them. However, closing the doors on your affairs doesn't mean they will leave you alone and won't manufacture tales about you. When you are blessed, those who hate you without cause will be too many to count, and too futile to try and counter. Let God do it for you.

6.6 INFIDELITY

Infidelity is forbidden in the scriptures, but it is also one of the most prominent marriage breakers for several reasons: man is often described as a gregarious animal, with fleeting interests, especially in intimacy issues. This is true to a large extent: his interest in physical relationship with his wife peaks on the honeymoon night and it takes God's Grace and love for his wife to sustain it through child-rearing and ageing. In contrast a wife's love for her husband and desire for physical relationship are on the rise, although that also often peaks when children start to arrive. Secondly, as both spouses rise in their careers, they become exposed to a wide range of intrusive temptations and pressures which the wife is often better at resisting. A husband who is seeking a divorce is likely having an affair already, while the wife is more likely to seek divorce based on irreconcilable differences.

A man's commitment to a marital relationship tends to obey the law of diminishing returns: courtship is hot, first sexual encounter is heavenly and, without strong self-control, quest for new experience is real. The problem is exaccrbatcd by thc incrcasingly largc population of aggrcssivc, socially and economically empowered, married and unmarried women out there waiting to lure him away from his marriage. Absentee dads are especially vulnerable; husbands who are closely involved in homecare and parenting, creating a conducive home environment are less likely to flirt. The wife has a lot to do in retaining the interest of her partner in the relationship. She should be at her physical best at all times; provide sexual and emotional satisfaction, even when she has no desire for it; she should not make the mistake of replacing her husband with the children; she should strive to cater specially for his interest, from food to physical relationship. The temptation to flirt is also real for women, especially when they are in an abusive relationship. For example, a woman who struggles to make ends meet may be susceptible to the advances of some 'money bag', or a boss at work who is in a position to enhance her financial status. It is interesting to note that husbands who flirt are totally intolerant of promiscuous wives and, even after divorce and with him being comfortable in new relationship, he could still be insanely jealous of seeing his wife with any other man.

Husbands must be able to provide economic security, physical security, sexual and emotional satisfaction for their wives. A husband who accepts the lifetime commitment model of marriage and is mindful of the potentially devastating effect of marriage breakup on his partner and children will strive hard to resist temptations that could end his marriage. Wives need to take their responsibilities to their family very seriously and this should supercede other commitments. Some women commit most of their energy and time in pursuing their primary interests at the expense of their responsibilities to their husbands, children and home.

Most men who flirt are not looking for a new wife, they start by simply looking for fun, conquest, or responding to the advances of an external aggressor. This is why they go to great lengths concealing their tracks initially. However, the illicit partner has a different agenda: she may be single, in an abusive relationship, or simply looking for 'greener grass', and she has a variety of potent instruments at her disposal to achieve her desired goal. Some men are wise enough to quickly realize the implications of their action and retreat but many become captured and sucked in: they either try to force their wives to accept the sharing model or start looking for excuses to walk out of their marriages. However, for many women in such an illicit relationship, sharing is merely a means to an end, the goal is complete take-over. In line with Christian values, both husband and wife should strive to resist temptations and uphold the commandment "thou shalt not covet", a moral imperative against infidelity.

6.7 ABUSE

The traditional concept of abuse/domestic violence in marriage implies physical assault but the scope has increased widely to include psychological abuse and maltreatment in any form: verbal abuse, nagging, neglect, humiliation, emotional stressing, domination, control, harassment, incessant criticism, etc. By far many more women suffer abuse in marriage than men. However, abuse is gender neutral and the dynamics vary between families. Children also suffer from various forms of abuse. Domestic abuse often escalates from threats and verbal abuse to violence and, while physical injury may be the most obvious danger, the emotional and psychological consequences of domestic abuse can be equally severe and devastating. Emotionally abusive relationships can destroy self-confidence, self-esteem, and can lead to anxiety and depression, loneliness, helplessness, and even suicide. Indicators of abuse include fear of your partner, having to watch what to do or say in order to avoid controversy, or feeling good being alone. A lot of people (women in particular) decide to device coping mechanisms because the options are equally fearful and also due to the societal stigma that single women suffer, but such people should realize that persistent abuse is 'killing me softly' and seek help promptly before they go under. Abuse of children can also lead to serious consequences, especially when the husband is the abuser and the wife feels helpless. Most children try to cope with abuse until they leave home but research and testimonies have shown that the psychological consequences in later life can be devastating and permanent.

6.8 DIVORCE

Divorce becomes inevitable when a couple lacks values and understanding of the meaning of commitment, loyalty, mutual adjustment, responsibility and the will to work together to sustain the family-united. Marriage is a lifetime commitment made between two people, to care and support each other, to fulfill their goals and objectives, to jointly parent the children and grow the family wealth, and to jointly manage issues. A family that is united by love is a family that will endure and overcome trying circumstances. Love, trust, commitment, selflessness, unity and perseverance are the key elements of a successful marriage. When one partner is self-centered, domineering, controlling, the relationship is doomed.

Many new couples think marriage is a bliss and their love boat will be smooth sailing. This is never true, and the misconception leads them to abandon the ship at the first sign of rough weather. Your spouse, no matter how wonderful they seem during courtship, is not perfect, neither are you. Unless couples develop the strategy of addressing problems, not the imperfections of their spouses, a marriage is bound to fail. Many other factors that can lead to the breakdown of a marriage have been discussed above. Many couples have disagreements and make up, until one day they fall apart for good. Divorce is a traumatic experience for most couples and can leave scars that last a lifetime, hence it should be absolutely a last resort. Marriage breakup has very complex and far-reaching consequences which most couples do not anticipate or comprehend until it is too late. Many issues can lead up to the collapse of a marriage, notably, selfishness/self-centeredness, financial problems, external interference, and infidelity. Your partner comes with a baggage of faults and inadequacies, just like you. It is selfish therefore for one to expect the other to do all the necessary adjustment: both of you have a lot of adjustments to make. The same is true of dealing with the varieties of issues that will inevitably arise in your marital life. It is quite common for either (usually the husband) to claim the last say on all issues: it is a potent recipe for failure, both of you have enormous resources and potentials which need to be fully integrated to get the best results.

Mismanagement of family wealth is a major cause of failed marriages, especially when one (usually the husband) is the dominant source, and this is the main reason why wives strive to retain some financial independence. While there are legal instruments of adjudication in the developed countries, there are very few mitigation options in many developing countries. It is not unusual for the wife to be sent out of a matrimonial home with nothing. Even in the developed world, many women shy away from taking advantage of legal options because of the cost, stress, endless court procedures, negative publicity, and the fear of the unknown, especially what happens to her children. Fortunately, many couples now seek the help of family lawyers who can help sort out the disengagement process with as little acrimony as possible. Most laws insist on separation for up to three years in the hope that there could be reconciliation. However, either partner may be in a new relationship within a few months, and may be under pressure to pursue a divorce rather than reconciliation.

Many marriages end in divorce because a spouse is oblivious of the wise saying "if the grass is greener on the other side, this means it is time to wet yours". There is absolutely no guarantee that a second marriage will work for either of you. In fact, statistics show that 45-50% of first marriages end in divorce, 70% of second, and 80% of third. The decreasing chances of success of serial monogamy are due to the fact that divorced partners in new relationships now have an opportunity to compare what they had with what the now have, and, quite often, it leads to regret. This explains why some divorced couples (around 13%) eventually come back together.

Infidelity is the most common cause of breakdown of marriages that end in divorce. Although it is condemnable and cannot be justified on any ground, there could be precipitous reasons: failed expectations at the home front; lack of emotional intimacy; incompatible sexual appetite; financial stresses (especially the wife). Money is perhaps the second major stressor in marriages:

not enough (and it hardly ever is) to meet the family's primary needs. Inequity between partners in terms of access can lead to power struggle and strain a marriage to breaking point. Other major stressors which often lead to divorce are lack of bonding, partnership and communication, endless quarrels and arguments, either partner becoming increasingly careless in his/her appearance, abusive relationship, unrealistic expectations, lack of mutually fulfilling sexual intimacy, inequitable sharing of family responsibilities. Another potential marriage breaker is the unpreparedness of one partner for marriage: people often decide to get married because of family or societal pressure, or as a result of pregnancy. Also, quite often, a partner (usually the male) would rather continue in a non-committal relationship indefinitely while his partner is increasingly anxious about ageing, and the decision to marry may have been the result of coercion by partner or family.

The effect of divorce on children is potentially devastating, in particular, the younger ones. Children often develop a core need for emotional unity, consistency and continuity and separation/divorce of parents inevitably brings considerable distress and instability. Even those who have left home look forward to a happy, stable home to which they can always return and feel welcome. Apart of the pain of the loss of a cherished memory of a happy home, divorce procedures are nearly always toxic and leave everyone including the children severely wounded and traumatized. Many children never recover and the scars persist in their adulthood. Divorce affects children in many ways: witnessing altercations that often precede divorce, coping with the stress and bitterness of the typically long process of divorce, having to adjust to living with only one parent and oscillating between two different households, having to adjust to step parents and a new home environment which may be abusive, all create stresses which interfere with normal development and behavior, notably peer relationships, stress management, aggression, education.

The effect on children is to some extent age-dependent: while teenagers can cope and quickly adjust to a new situation, the younger ones are extremely vulnerable. According to psychologists, children under ten are usually very dependent: their parents are all in all, and divorce fractures their comfort zone, creating two negative family units between which they must learn to transit back and forth while they learn the politics of relating amicably to two people at war. The overall impact on the child is retrogressive. The situation is often worse if the custodian partner decides to remarry before they leave home, which brings in a third stressor that they have to cope with. On the contrary, divorce tends to promote aggression and accelerate the independence of the adolescent who is already less dependent on parents, more self-sustaining and self-sufficient, with a circle of potentially supportive friends. However, it tends to impact negatively on their confidence in the marriage institution. Statistics show that persons who are the children of divorced parents are slightly less likely to marry, and when they do marry are much more likely to divorce, four times more than the children of couples who are not divorced.

Divorce should not be an option in marriage: the ideal advice is '*never quit; winners never quit and quitters never win*'. However, the reality is that it can be dangerous or even deadly to coerce two people into staying together who have decided that they couldn't. In some situations, divorce may be inevitable, for example, making a mistake (or mischoice) from the start, blindness to red flags during courtship, or inability to make the mutual sacrifice of adjustment. The experience of Jane (not real name) is a common example: she and her husband met at university and courted for five years before getting married but the marriage fell apart within four months. She admits that there were alarm bells during courtship including short temper, flirtatious tendencies and lack of enthusiasm during preparations for the marriage, but she didn't hear them, she kept getting good at deluding herself that everything would be ok. There are very many Janes who end up in abusive marriage but relatively few have the courage to leave the marriage: statistics show that around a third of married couples admit they are actively unhappy but unable to leave, but Jane did, and within three months she met Dick (not the real name) who she married after nine months of courtship, and they have had a happy marriage for nearly a decade, with two loving children and a vibrant life. However, the problem of Jane was relatively easy: there was no child between them. Things become more complicated when children are involved and custody battles can be intense and hurtful. The complication is even more when two separated people who have custody of the children decide to marry, thereby creating a new 'blended family" which has its own potentially serious issues. Divorce is bitter, but sometimes each partner learns lessons in reappraisal and rediscovery which help them to avoid the same pitfalls in new relationships.

Life after divorce can be traumatic, especially for women. Many find it difficult to let go while others feel very bitter and hurt by dashed hopes and dreams or the abuse that they have endured; they become deeply suspicious of virtually everyone around them and, for Christians, it can be a major test of faith. Singleness after divorce can be traumatic and the healing process can be slow, often leading to rushing into another relationship (rebound). There are many Christian and professional counseling resources that can help people in such situation to pick up the pieces and move on. There are also many Christian and community support groups that could help in the process of recovery. Rushing into another relationship is hardly ever the answer, and this explains why second relationships have a higher chance of failure. Nevertheless, a failed marriage does not mean that you are a failure, it just means that you need to re-examine and re-evaluate yourself, your past mistakes; you need to re-discover a 'new you', more mature, realistic and pragmatic about relationships. In any new relationship you will still face the same issues and problems that erode a relationship, and your chances of success second time around would depend on your ability to positively apply the lessons learnt in the previous marriage. It is vital to hold on firmly to one's faith, turn your grief into His glory, and find comfort and encouragement in the words of Betsy St. Amant: "Whatever pain you're feeling today, whatever hurt you're confused about how to acknowledge, look through the shadows for the light. Look past the divorce papers or the tombstone or the scars, and focus on the One who held you in those dark moments. His fingerprints are all over our worst days. Not because He caused them, but because He observed them. And not from the front row or from the wings—but from center stage, right beside you."

Core Values for Growing a Marriage from Good to Great, Built to Last a Lifetime

"Marriage can move from good to great, built to last a lifetime when two imperfect people come together, work together, win together, lose together, build dreams together, and refuse to give up on each other despite formidable odds." — Afonja

"Love isn't always perfect. It isn't a fairytale or a storybook. And it doesn't always come easy. Love is overcoming obstacles, facing challenges, fighting to be together, holding on and never letting go. It is a short word, easy to spell, difficult to define, and impossible to live without. Love is work, but most of all, Love is realizing that every hour, every minute and every second was worth it because you did it together."
— Unknown

"The couples that are meant to be, are the ones who go through everything that is meant to tear them apart, and come out even stronger." ---Unknown

"Life had broken her; just as it had broken him. But when they got together, their pieces became whole. And they continued on their journey together , mended as one."
— Steve Maraboli

"Marriage is like music. Both are playing different instruments and different parts, but as long as you are playing from the same sheet music, you can create something beautiful." — Fiercemarriage

"Marriage is a thousand little things... It's giving up your right to be right in the heat of argument. It's forgiving another when they let you down. It's loving someone enough to step down so they can shine. It's friendship. It's being a Cheerleader and trusted confidant. It's a place of forgiveness that welcomes one home, and arms they can run to in the midst of a storm. It' grace." — Darlene Schacht

"It takes three to make love, not two: you, your spouse, and God. Without God people only succeed in bringing out the worst in one another. Lovers who have nothing else to do but love each other soon find there is nothing else. Without a central loyalty life is unfinished." — Fulton J. Sheen

"Love is composed of a single soul inhabiting two bodies." — Aristotle, philosopher

"A happy marriage is about three things: memories of togetherness, forgiveness of mistakes and a promise never to give up on each other". — Surabhi Serendra

" A great relationship doesn't happen because of the love you had in the beginning, but how well you continue building love until the end – Unknown

"No relationship is all sunshine, but two people can share one umbrella and survive the storm together".— Lovethings

"Treat marriage like a diamond necklace; if broken, fix it, but do not throw it away." — Matshona Dhliwayo

"Marriage is a great blessing, but it can be a great lesson" — Ernest Agyemang Yeboah

"We're all a little weird. And life is a little weird. And when we find someone whose weirdness is compatible with ours, we join up with them and fall into mutually satisfying weirdness–and call it love–true love." — Robert Fulghum

"Trouble in a marriage is like monsoon water accumulating on a flat roof. You don't realize it's up there, but it gets heavier and heavier, until one day, with a great crash, the whole roof falls in on your head." — Salman Rushdie, Joseph Anton

"When a man loves a woman she becomes his weakness. When a woman truly loves a man he becomes her strength. This is called exchange of power --- Pinecrest

"There is no more lovely, friendly, and charming relationship, communton or company than a good marriage."— Martin Luther

"Relationship math suggests that It is rare for two people to enter marriage and one person is to blame for everything that goes wrong." — Johnnie Dent Jr.

"Marriage is a full-time job; wooing is your application, courtship your interview, engagement your job offer, and honeymoon, your orientation." — Matshona Dhliwayo

"Be calm when your wife yells at you, calmer when she chastens you, but be terrified when she ignores you." — Matshona Dhliwayo

"You kids were all in college, and I suddenly saw that I was stuck alone with a man who, all those years later, was still wanting me to be someone I wasn't." — Barbara Delinsky

"When we get to the end of our lives together, the house we had, the cars we drove, the things we possessed won't matter. What will matter is that I had you and you had me. " — Pinecrest

"Love has nothing to do with what you are expecting to get, only with what you are expecting to give - which is everything." — Katharine Hepburn

7 Great marriages can last a lifetime

7.1 INTRODUCTION

A little boy was asked about his understanding of love, and his response was fascinating: he described love as a relationship between an old couple who know so much about each other and still care so much about each other. This is in fact a precise definition of a couple that has succeeded in building a great marriage, destined to last a lifetime. Marriages can last decades and yet be loaded with problems sowed and nurtured in the earlier years. The relationship may be largely devoid of mutual love, empathy, commitment and partnership. The relationship becomes increasingly vulnerable as children leave home: one partner may be pursuing a lifelong passion while the other stays home miserable and lonely. This kind of relationship often ends up in divorce even at this late stage of their marital life.

7.2 THE FINAL YEARS

By the end of thirty years of marital life, the children have left home and you are back to where you started from, but with lots of experience gained from navigating through life, family and career issues and raising children. Count yourself lucky if your marriage is still intact: statistics show that only 25% of married couples celebrate their 35th anniversary and 5% are still together after fifty years. It should be noted however that divorce is not the only cause of the low longevity of marriages: most people, especially men who get married at the age of 25–35 years die before their 50th wedding anniversary. If you are lucky and both have good health, you could live another 25 – 30 years after children have left home, and it should be the best segment of your marriage. Those who have the grace tend to enjoy the fruits of their labor, watching the blossomed tree, warmed by their love and affection. It is a time for reflection on the pleasures and struggles of life together. Recounting the tales of their years together makes old age pleasurable in-spite of the wrinkles, loss of hair, loss of hearing and other health challenges. Those who are lucky are surrounded by family and friends but this is becoming increasingly rare in view of the isolationism of the modern world. It is a time to pursue mutual interests such as joining clubs and programs for seniors.

Couples who are so lucky start to spend a lot of time together, reflecting on the tortuous journey: courtship, marriage, career, the challenges they surmounted, hard times, milestones, pleasant memories, travels, etc., taking care of each other especially when health issues start to multiply. Couples may engage in light intellectual work, go to movies, take regular walk, eat out. Perhaps the most fulfilling is to sit back and watch your children raise their own families, often dealing with the same parenting issues you had with them. It gives you even greater pleasure if you are still able to help in anyway, like minding and school runs. Couples now live into their eighties, thanks to the increasingly effective medical care, and it is not unusual to find couples who are still together in their late nineties. In those last twenty years or so you will hardly see one without the other due to the togetherness developed in the earlier years, and of course the new realities. When the inevitable happens and one partner passes away it is quite common for the other to follow, often within days. Science explains this common phenomenon as broken heart syndrome: the death of a spouse is one of the most stressful things that can happen to a person, especially when they have been together for decades. Apart from the shock of losing a long-term partner and best friend, the aged body is a lot more frail and the stress may be too much to handle. However, when one survives, families usually provide support but loneliness could be a major issue since younger family members are usually busy, even though they may hire service providers. This is why serviced apartments and special homes for seniors are becoming increasingly popular because they have access to good care and the opportunity to interact with other seniors while family can still help financially.

It is vital however that couples prepare well in their earlier years for this last phase of their lives. Apart from forging a close relationship in the earlier years, they need to ensure that they have decent financial resources. Although many modern societies have various support programs for seniors such as social security benefits, medicare, tax relief, the need for personal funds especially for health care is still substantial and, in many cases, families are not in a position to help. If couples made good investments in the early years, they can relax and live a reasonably comfortable life.

7.3   COMPLACENCY

Love between partners must progress steadily from genuine to intense and stable for it to last. Studies have found that couples that appear to be strongly affectionate at the start are more likely to divorce than those who display less affection but grow steadily in their relationship. Couples whose marriages begin in romantic bliss (often referred to as Hollywood romance) are particularly divorce-prone because such intensity is too hard to maintain. It is easy for couples to become complacent about their relationship in the process of growing careers and families, and if couples have become used to individualism and little communication in earlier years, it is difficult to correct in the last stage of life together, when partnership, mutual support and rich communication skills are crucial. It is also easy for each partner to take the other for granted and both need to work hard to sustain interest in each other and nurture common interests which can keep them busy through this last stage of life, like recreation, charity work, light social and intellectual activities. Nothing ends life and relationships at this stage faster than idleness and loneliness in a relationship that had been devoid of communication in earlier years. It is also important to note that men who had been flirtatious in earlier years will probably remain active right to the end. Furthermore, they are potential victims of exploitation by younger women, and this explains why some men walk away from mature marriages to start life with women younger than their daughters. Wives also need to know that they must not devote all their time, attention and affection to the children (and careers) at the expense of their partners in the earlier years. It is always too late to try and make amends in the last stages of your life together.

7.4   SELFISHNESS

Career growth and bringing up children can be so taxing that everything else is relegated to the background. This is a potentially lethal marriage killer. Some men become so involved in club activities that they spend most of their spare time away from home in the earlier years. Such men find it difficult to readjust in later years. While most wives adjust to the demands of recreational activities of their partners in the earlier years due largely to the compensative effect of children, it usually becomes unbearable in the last years. Women have been known to walk away from marriages of over forty years because they could no longer cope with loneliness due to their partner's social activities. It is vital therefore that couples develop mutual social and recreational interest in earlier life that can keep them busy through the last years. Even couples that did not succeed in doing this often try to make up by joining senior fitness and social club activities.

7.5   BECOMING GRANDPARENTS

Each couple should expect to be the foundation for many subsequent generations. The birth of the first child sets that off and as soon as he/she gets married and has a child, another generation is born. The gradual increase in number is part of God's Divine order, it is a process of maturation that turns one person into dozens depending on the number of the first set of children and the age of the couple before they pass on. It is a fulfilling and joyful period that rewards all investments in the union, and is worth waiting for together. Welcoming the second set of infants into the world often coincides with retirement thus allowing the couple enough time and energy to support and bond with their children and grandchildren. School run and school activities keep grandparents active and joyful as they share experiences with other grandparents. Sometimes they are the backbones for vacation activities and special celebrations such as Thanksgiving, Christmas and New Year. Of course, the birthday of each family member is also one to celebrate grandparents as everyone acknowledges their roles. Grandparents also play a significant parenting role when any of their children becomes a single parent or for some reason is unable to look after his/her children.

7.6   HARVEST TIME: IT IS NOT ALL ABOUT MONEY

A union is great not simply because of the number of years of marriage, the number of children and grandchildren and the amount of wealth but by the level of marital satisfaction, intimacy, passion and commitment to each other. These are enriched by each person's total life satisfaction, a much wider concept to which marital satisfaction contributes substantially. Professional accomplishments, good health, decent living, accomplished children and grandchildren, companionship etc. all provide the joy and are outcomes of a great marriage. There is nothing more satisfying than spending your last years together sharpening your spiritual standing with God and praying for your children, infused with pleasurable recreation and relaxation. In the age of digital communication, some parents pray regularly by Skype with their children even when they are thousands of miles away. It is also a rich source of joy to travel around and spend time with your children's families or host them in your home.

7.7   PREPARING FOR THE INEVITABLE

Couples should expect the inevitable, the departure of one to the great beyond. The tendency is for this to be spaced. In only a few cases will a couple pass on within days, weeks or months of each other. Couples tend to shy away from discussing this "inevitability" yet it is very useful if a surviving partner knows the wishes of the other. Time should be spent discussing post departure arrangements for the surviving partner, disposal of assets and the funeral arrangements. It is quite common for each partner to take all vital decisions about his/her funeral, including choosing burial site, order of ceremony and favorite songs. Couples should develop individual or joint legal wills detailing how they wish their assets to be disposed of but, most importantly, a couple should define their legacy and how to perpetuate it.

8.   REFERENCES AND BIBLIOGRAPHY

APA (2019). "Parenting". apa.org.

Archer, Julian,(2014*). Help, I 've Been Blessed! How to stop God's blessings from becoming curses.* (See also faith-vs-finance.org).

Bailey, Nathan (2019). "Christian Courtship – an annotated bibliography". polynate.net/books.

Bailey, Nathan (1997-2010). "Dating vs Courtship Parts 1 – 8". polynate.net/books/courtship/.

Balswick, J. and Judith (2014). The family: A Christian Perspective on the Contemporary Home. Baker Academic.

Barber, B. K. (Ed.) (2002). *Intrusive parenting: How psychological control affects children and adolescents.* American Psychological Association Press.

Berger, J. (2016). *Invisible Influence: The Hidden Forces that Shape Behavior*. Simon and Schuster Paperbacks.

Bhikkhu, P. (2000). *Love your children the right way*. Buddhanikhom Chiang Mai.

Brainyquote (2019) Marriage Quotes. brainyquote.com.

Brann, Deanna (2016). *Reluctantly Related: Secrets To Getting Along With Your Mother-in-Law or Daughter-in-Law*. Ambergris Publishing.

Brereton, S. L. (2016). Dating vs Courtship; and Everything in Between. seanlbrereton.com.

Butterfield Fox (2018). *In My Father's House: A New View of How Crime Runs in the Family*. Alfred A. Knopf/Penguin.

Chandra P. (2011). "Is midlife crisis real?" Prevention News – India Today.

News.

Chapman, Annie (2004). *The Mother-in-Law Dance: Can two women love the same man and still get along?* Harvest House Publishers.

Chernoff, S. (2015). "Midlife Crisis? Let's break it down." sethchernoff.com.

Christian Courtship (2019). "Christian Courtship". Christian-courtship.com. Accessed 2/15/2019.

Cicurel, Deborah, (2015) "17 important qualities to look for in your life partner". metro.co.uk.

Credit Suisse (2013). *Global Wealth Report, October 2013.* credit-suisse.com.

Dalrymple, Timothy (2011). "What really is the institution of marriage"? patheos.com.

Daugherty, J., and C. Copen (2016). *Trends in Attitudes About Marriage, Childbearing and Sexual Behavior: United States 2002 - 2013.* National Health Statistics Reports No 92, March 17, 2016.

DeArmond, Deb (2015). Related by Chance, Family by Choice: Transforming Mother-in-Law and Daughter-in-Law Relationships. Kregel Publications.

De Botton, Allain (2017) "The true hard work of love and relationships". onbeing.org.

Duggar, J & M. (2018). "How is courtship different than dating?" Institute in Basic Life Principles. iblp,org.

Erickson, D. L (2014) "Stages of Development – Learning Theories" in Learning Theories. learning-theories.com.

Evans, Jimmy and Allan Kelsey (2016). *Strengths Based Marriage: Build a*

Stronger Relationship by Understanding Each other's Gifts.

Evans, Jimmy (2012). *Marriage on the rock: God's design for your dream marriage.* XO Publishing.

Evans, Jimmy (2014). *Our Secret Paradise: Seven secrets for building a secure and satisfying marriage.* XO Publishing.

Family Life Today (2019). familylifetoday.com.

Fertel, Mort (2019). "7 Steps to Fixing Your Marriage". marriagemax.com.

Fileta, Debra (2019). "How the Courtship vs Dating Debate is Changing". Christian-courtship.com.

Finkel, E. J. (2017). *The All-or-Nothing Marriage: How the best Marriages Work.* Duton/Penguin.

Frank D. Fincham and Steven R. H. Beach, "I Say a Little Prayer for You: Praying for Partner Increases Commitment in Romantic Relationships," Journal of Family Psychology 28, no. 5 (2014): 587-593.

Fulgum, Robert (1993). *All I really need to know I learned in Kindergarten: Uncommon thoughts on common things.* Random House Publishing Group.

Gallup (2011). *Worldview.* gallup.com

Gottman, J. (2015). *The Seven Principles for Making Marriage Work.* Harmony Books.

Graham, Elizabeth (2010). *Mothers-in-law vs. Daughters-in-law: Let There Be Peace.* Beacon Hill Press.

Hagee, Diana (). *Ten qualities of nurturing intimacy.*

Hagee, John & Diana (2007). *What every man wants in a woman/What every woman wants in a man.*jhm.org.

HageeMinistries (2019). "Relationships". jhm.org. Accessed 2/26/2019.

Hanselman, Daniel and Jacquelin (2017). *Silencing the accuser: Restoration of Your Birthright.* God's Foundation Builders.

Higbee, Garret (2018). "The Couple that Prays Together Stays Together." forthefamily.org.

Jakes, T. D. (2006). *Not Easily Broken.* Warner Faith Hachette Book Group U.S.A.

Jory, B. (2018) *Cupid on Trial – What we Learn About Love When Loving Gets Tough.* Foxford International Books and Media.

Keller, J. Timothy (2015). *The meaning of Marriage Study Guide: A Vision for Married and Single People.* . Zondervan.

Kennedy, Talia (2019). "The Difference Between Courtship and Dating". datingtips.match.com.

Kurup, R. K., & P. A Kurup (2003). "Hypothalamic digoxin: Central role in conscious perception, neuroimmunoendocrine integration and coordination of cellular function – relation to hemispheric dominance". *Medical Hypotheses,* 60(2), 243-257.

Ludy, Leslie & Eric (2009). When God Writes Your Love Story: The Ultimate Guide to Guy/Girl Relationships. Multinomah Books.

Meyer, Joyce (2015). *Power of words: What you say can change your life.* Faithword.

Nathaniel M. Lambert, Frank D. Fincham, Dana C. LaVallee, and Cicely W. Brantley, "Praying Together and Staying Together: Couple Prayer and Trust," Psychology of Religion and Spirituality 4, no. 1 (2012): 1-9 (2).

Mackay , H. (1997). Generations: Baby boomers, their parents and their children. Sydney, Australia: Pan MacMillan.

Marriage.com (2019) "Five facets of the true meaning of marriage". marriage.com.

Marx, Karl (1867). *The Communist Manifesto, The Eighteenth Brumaire of Louis Bonaparte and Capital.*

NASEM (2016). " Parenting Knowledge, Attitudes and Practices". In *Parenting Matters: Supporting Parents of Children Ages 0-8*. National Academy of Sciences, Engineering and Medicine; Division of Behavioral and Social Sciences and Education. National Academies Press.

Neuman, F. (2013). "The Anatomy of Dating". psychologytoday.com.

Newman, Judith (2017). *To Siri with Love*. HarperCollins Publishers.

Niehuis, S. (2008). Dating and courtship. In J. T. Sears (Ed.), The Greenwood encyclopedia of love, courtship, and sexuality through history, Vol. 6: The modern world (pp. 57-60). Westport, CT: Greenwood Press.

Peterson, G. W. and Bush, K. R. (2013). Handbook of *Marriage and the Family*. Springer.

Popenoe David and Whitehead, Barbara Dafoe (2004)'Ten important findings on marriage and choosing a partner- Helpful facts for young adults in National Marriage Project.

Psychology Today (2019). "Parenting". psychologytoday.com.

RCCG (2019). TOD singles and youth training module 2. The Redeemed Christian Church of God, Netherlands. rccgtod.org.

Rogers, Adrian (2016.) "Marriage is from heaven". YouTube [#2077].

Rogers, Adrian (2016). "Five Ways to be a Successful Husband". Youtube [#2229].

Sapirstein, Milton (1963). *Paradoxes of Everyday Life: A psychoanalyst's interpretations of the patterns of conflict in human behavior*. Fawcett Publications.

Scott, B. M. and Shwartz, M. A. (2007) Marriages and Families, New Jersey: Pearson Education Inc.

Shuler, Clarence (2013). Keeping Your Wife Your Best Friend: A Practical Guide for Husbands. Building Lasting Relationships Publishing House, Colorado Springs. clarenceshuler.com.

Shuler, Clarence (2019). "Couples who pray together".

Strauss, M. A. (1979) Intra-family conflict and violence: The Conflict Tactics Scales, Journal of Marriage and the Family, Vol 41, 75-88.

Strauss M. A. (1990) The conflict tactics: scales and its critics: an evaluation and new data on the validity and reliability in Strauss M. A and Gelles R. J. Physical Violence (eds.) Physical Violence in American Families: Risk Factors and Adaptation to Violence in 8,145 Families, (pages 49-73) New Brunswick, N. J. Transaction.

Stravrinides, P. and Nikiforou, M. (2013). "Parenting Challenges, Practices and Cultural Influences." In book: Parenting : Challenges, Practices and Cultural Influences, Chapter 3, pp. 59-82. Nova Science.

Stritof, S. (2019). "The Physical and Relational Benefits of Frequent Sex". verywellmind.com.

Strong, B., DeVault, C., and T. Cohen (2011). The Marriage and Family Experience: *Intimate Relationships in a Changing Society*. Wandsworth Cengage Learning.

Swindol, Charles (2001). *Wisdom for the way: Wise words for busy people.* J. Countryman/Thomas Nelson.

Thornton, A., Axinn, W., and Yu Xie (2007). *Marriage and Cohabitation.* University of Chicago Press.

Tung,Tong Pui (2007) Romantic Relationship: Love Styles, TriangularLove and Relationship Satisfaction, City University of Hong Kong (Online).

Turner, Adrienna (2009). "The day begins with Christ". Arthur House.

Twenge, J. M. *et. al.* (2014). "Declines in Sexual Frequency among American Adults". Archives of Sexual Behavior. Vol. 46(8), pp 2389-2401.

Venugopal, Veen (2014). *The Mother-in-Law: The other woman in Your Marriage.* Penguin.

Waite, Linda J and Gallaher, Maggie (2001) *The case for marriage: why people are happier and better financially.* Doubleday.

Warnes, Brian (2002) God's Best: Choosing a Marriage Partner. en.wikipedia.org/wiki/Courtship.

Wikipedia (2019). "Midlife Crisis". Wikipedia.org.

Young, Ben and Samuel Adams (2004): "What is the difference between courting and dating". In *Ten Commandments of Dating.* Thomas Nelson.

Youssef, M. (2016). "Parenting our children's hearts." ltw.org.

Youssef, M. (2016). "Believing God for the family." ltw.org.